JOHN CAMPBELL

Rediscovery
of an
Arts & Crafts Architect

Alan Powers

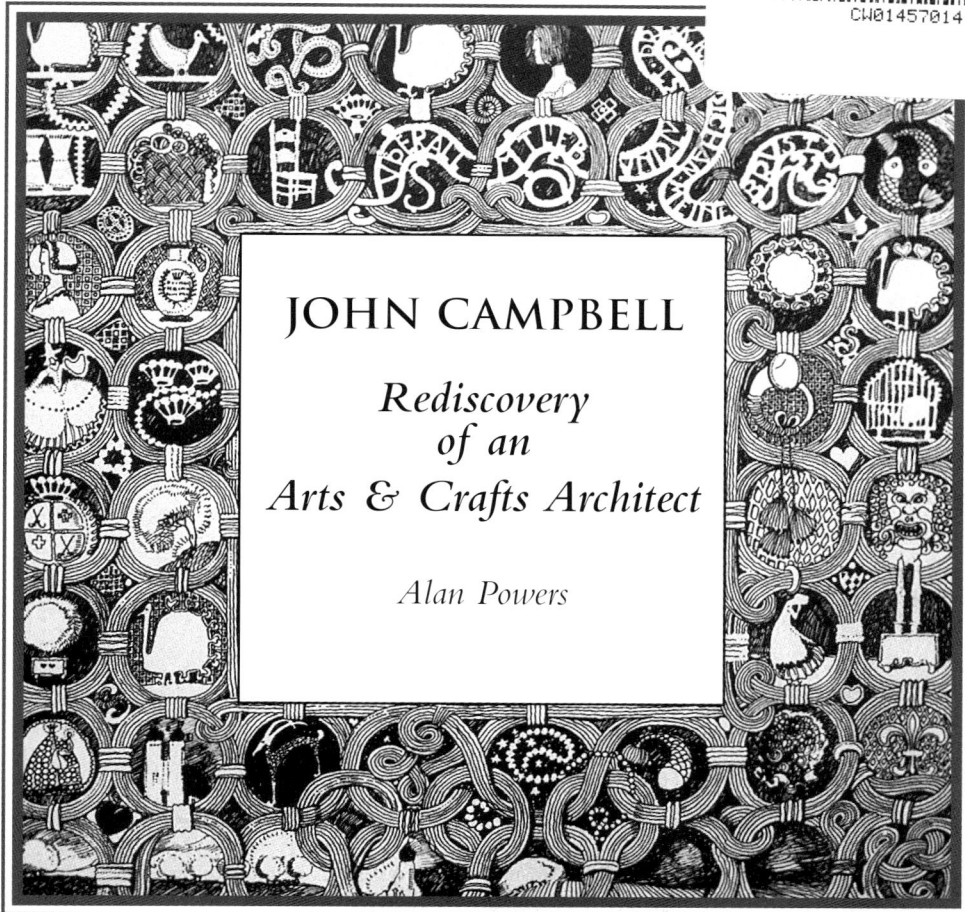

THE PRINCE OF WALES'S INSTITUTE OF ARCHITECTURE

FOREWORD

Alan Crawford

Campbell & Pullich Haus Schikendanz, Berlin 1909, from **Innen-Dekoration***, 1909*

I FIRST CAME ACROSS John Campbell a few years ago, when I was working through early twentieth-century periodicals, trying to get a sense of the influence of Charles Rennie Mackintosh in Germany. In the pages of *Deutsche Kunst und Dekoration* for 1908 and 1909 I found illustrations of work by Campbell & Pullich of Berlin which struck me as very reminiscent of English Arts and Crafts work, particularly that of M.H. Baillie Scott. 'Interesting', I thought, 'what an odd name'. Then I consigned Campbell and Pullich to the crowded mental shelf of the things-you-would-like-to-know-more-about-but-you-know-you-never-will.

Some time later I read a very good PhD thesis by Catherine Gordon on Arts and Crafts architecture in the Cotswolds which included an account of the work of the firm Falconer, Baker & Campbell in and around Stroud in Gloucestershire in the 1920s. Campbell is a common enough name, and Stroud is a long way from Berlin, and I did not connect the two. But then Alan Powers told me that he had unearthed the drawings and papers of this very interesting architect, John Campbell, and things began to fall into place.

There used to be a simple Modernist narrative for architectural relationships between Britain and Germany in the first half of the twentieth century. It went like this: in the early twentieth century influence flowed from Britain to Germany, the homely matter-of-factness of British Arts and Crafts work helping to shape early German Modernism. Then, after the First World War and a decent interval, influence flowed from Germany to Britain in the form of fully-fledged Modernism and, in the 1930s, refugees from the Third Reich, some of whom stayed in Britain while others moved on to the United States.

John Campbell's career was itself a kind of Anglo-German relationship. He went to Germany in 1902 and was offered a job on the strength of his experience in British interior design (the illustrations I saw in *Deutsche Kunst und Dekoration* were more closely tied to Britain than I knew). He was interned in Germany during the First World War. In 1918 he came back to England and worked in London and the Cotswolds (where he gave the Bear Inn Hotel at Rodborough Common a rather Germanic corner tower). But then he went back to Germany in 1928 and set up a practice in Berlin for the second time, only to return to England in 1931, where he worked until his death.

You might be tempted to try and fit Campbell's career into the larger art-historical narrative. But it does not work. For one thing, the story of his strange career does not follow a neat linear path. All his to-ing and fro-ing seems to have been a necessary restlessness, partly a romantic search for good work and a good place, partly a response to accidents (divorce, war, chance meetings in pubs). John Campbell was not very conscious of the larger patterns which art historians perceive.

And for another, his work remained rooted in his earliest inspiration, in British Arts and Crafts and the picturesque German vernacular that answered to Arts and Crafts tastes. The last major works of his career, Birchens Spring, Beaconsfield, Buckinghamshire of 1933-34 and the houses at Chapel Point, Mevagissey, Cornwall of 1935-38 are also, arguably, the finest of his designs. Their forms are bold and simple; massy like Ernest Gimson's work but not so obviously rough, severe like Voysey's but not so coy. Cleanness is perhaps the word. These houses extend the history and the meanings of the Arts and Crafts movement.

JOHN CAMPBELL AS A TEACHER

Ronald Leask

John Archibald Campbell, Architect, 1878 - 1947

M EETING THIS REMARKABLE MAN was a major factor in my development as a man and as an architect. At the outbreak of the war Campbell was recruited to work for the Ministry of Aircraft Production in London. He left his house in Cornwall and took digs in Kensington. With failing eyesight and engaged in mundane work, he struggled against depression. He was rescued from this slough by the then headmaster of Blundell's School, Neville Gorton, who invited him "to come and tell the boys about architecture". Under Gorton's inspired leadership the school had become a community that stressed individual excellence dedicated to Christian worship and the common good. Democracy was fostered by the abolition of fagging and the awarding of "colours" for achievement in the arts and sciences as well as for sport. There was a fine music and drama tradition and excellent workshops for the production of the practical and fine arts. Eric Gill had designed a stone altar that was built and carved in relief by the boys.

The two years at the school gave Campbell three gifts: the first, time to study and reflect; the second, contact with youth; and the third, his last pupil, myself. He set up an office on the first floor of the school workshops overlooking the playing fields and the Devon hills beyond. Despite the noise from the lathe and circular saw this room became a haven of calm. There was a comforting aroma compounded of cedar and pencil sharpenings, wine, tobacco and tweed. He made wooden toys, read extensively and prepared his lectures to the Sixth Form.

While at Blundell's he lost his right eye due to a bungled operation to remove a cataract. The Architectural Sixth was a branch of History Sixth and numbered ten boys. We were a very ordinary crowd with not many ideas on anything, let alone architecture. To our young minds he appeared as the complete "Professor" and because of his general untidiness and abstracted dignity, we nicknamed him "Shambles". Our first term was spent knocking two spare rooms in the workshop into our studio. In this way, we learnt by experience the elements of woodwork, masonry, plastering and decorating. Between the building efforts there were lectures on lettering, building construction and how to make a measured survey. With our studio complete, we started work in earnest by drawing up our tuck shop survey and attempting to design a single cell building, a village hall. Then we studied housing and how to assemble small volumes in plan, section and elevation. We were shown some of the limitations imposed by building regulations. As we worked in our studio, he worked in his office upstairs on "A Two Roomed House for A Millionaire", drawn in ink and coloured on stretched Watman paper. We did not then appreciate the philosophy behind the design but marvelled at the exquisite draughtsmanship of a one-eyed man. In fact, this work was a manifesto on the values he considered important to a truly human culture.

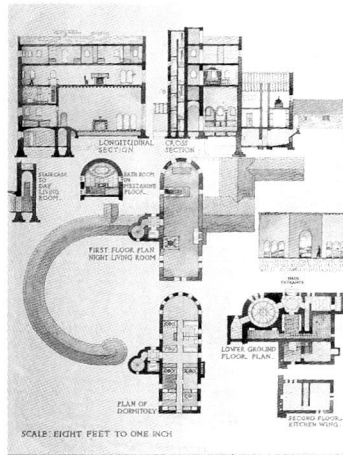

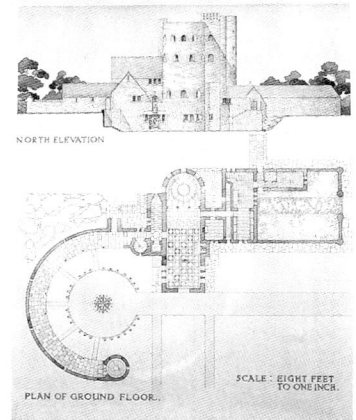

"A Two Roomed House for A Millionaire", 1943

He said that he had to spend time un-teaching us from the habitual and often narrow preconceptions of conventional society, so that he could "corrupt us"! We were not given a set task to be completed within a time limit, under supervision; instead he set each a task and left us to work at our own speed. Walking round the studio, looking over our shoulders, he would stop and talk quietly to an individual while the others worked on. Sometimes he would invite us all to gather round to hear him emphasize a particular point of general interest. He did not tell us exactly what to do, but roused in us a dissatisfaction with our efforts and working with this feeling, would employ the Socratic method of question and answer to lead us to overcome the difficulty for ourselves. One of us once asked, "what shall I do?" He replied, "you mean what shall I be?".

By the end of the first term we had given up all schoolboy tricks in the realisation that our form-master was a great man. Once inside our studio, we were in a special and privileged world outside the confines of school and its rules. We felt a kind of responsibility to this lonely old man, who looked so out of place in the school environment. We visited buildings in Tiverton and Exeter, made sketches and listened to his comments. Besides the instruction we received in our studio, Campbell gave talks on the history of architecture to the whole History Sixth. One of these developed his theory that if the Moors had won the battle of Tours and proceeded North to merge with the young Celtic civilisation in the West, a more vibrant culture, freed from the heavy hand of Rome, might have arisen. Because our studio was part of the workshops we were able to gain a first hand knowledge of stone and wood carving, carpentry, and modelling in clay, under the expert and kindly guidance of Harry Phillips and Willi Soukop. Three other boys and I carved figures of the four Evangelists in Portland stone, on a pulpit designed by Campbell to complement Eric Gill's altar in the school chapel.

Design for Blundell's School Library, c.1943, incorporating sculpture by Willi Soukop

Campbell and I left Blundell's at the same time and, accompanied by Walter Douglas, the master in charge of the History Sixth, went to Hoxton where we were engaged on the conversion of an old Board School building into a youth club for Holy Trinity Church. Father Bernard Walke, a high church Anglican, had met Campbell in Cornwall and recommended him to Holy Trinity.

While we were in Hoxton the V1 and V2 rockets descended on the city and we were privileged to share the wonderful spirit of the East Enders united in adversity. Campbell with his humour and cheerfulness formed a warm human rapport with everyone, irrespective of age, sex or class; a true "Gent" in every sense of the word. I left for military service and during one of my leaves, visited Chapel Point for the first time. The Campbell family were enjoying a summer holiday in a temporary hut built on the Point in preparation for the resumption of building work after the war. We shared food and drink, sang songs and enjoyed each others' company with the sparkle of the sea under the blue horizon. It was indeed an enchanted time and place enhanced by the gleaming white houses which seemed like castles in spite of their small size.

Returning from service with the Royal Marines in 1946, I joined Campbell in an office he had set up in Brompton Road, London. The intended Youth Club had been bombed to destruction and he had started again on the development of Chapel Point. *Country Life* had featured the three houses in two articles and these had attracted new clients. Frances, his wife, looked after the secretarial work and I helped as an unqualified assistant. We made a scale model of the complete development of Chapel Point that was accepted for the Summer Exhibition at the Royal Academy in 1947. The office was very busy with commissions that included the rebuilding of a bombed church, a house in Kenya, a rural settlement in the Western Isles, and various private houses.

Always a keen observer of current affairs, Campbell fulminated against the Allies' insistence on unconditional surrender and mourned the destruction, by fire-bombing, of many well known and loved German buildings. In spite of a very heavy work load with inadequate assistance, he found time to write an eloquent attack on the prefabricated house proposed by the Government as a solution to the post-war housing shortage. He argued that prefabrication was appropriate for structural components and fittings, but not for walls and roofs, which should be formed of traditional materials in the interests of permanence and Regional character. The Planning Application for the fourth house on Chapel Point, approved before the war, was refused. Work started on a beautifully written and illustrated appeal which was completed and posted in Mevagissey on the evening of the 18th August 1947. Walking back to the hut on the Point, where his wife and son lay sleeping, he missed his footing in the dark and fell to his death on the rocks below the Cliff. The appeal was successful.

The following is an extract from the report of the Inspector W.A.Devereux, FRIBA.

"The general standard and layout of the development at Chapel Point envisages an exceptional example of coastal planning, which if carried to its completion by the appellant would fit well into the landscape and be a satisfactory small scale development complete in itself."

When working for John Campbell during his last years, he often urged me to leave him and study modern methods and techniques unfamiliar to him. After his death I acted on his advice and was accepted into the second year course at the Architectural Association school on the strength of the portfolio built up under his tutelage. At that early stage in my architectural development I did not appreciate the depth of his vision.

The A.A. school immediately after the war was an exiting place. The average age of the students was about 24, many having served under fire during the hostilities. There were 120 in our year. Scandinavia was the design inspiration, followed closely by the Bauhaus and Le Corbusier. The school had a rugby club and a flourishing dramatic society. All were inspired with the aim of building a new and vibrant Britain. There were devoted tutors, most of whom were practising architects. We had visits from Le Corbusier and Frank Lloyd Wright. John Summerson, Ove Arup, Felix Samuely and Walter Segal were in almost daily attendance.

My Campbell-influenced designs were ridiculed as old fashioned, but I received encouragement from John Brandon-Jones who introduced us to the works of Philip Webb, Norman Shaw and Mackintosh and urged us to look deeper than the fashions of the moment.

Many of these fashions have proved ephemeral, but Campbell's vision continues to inspire, because it speaks of the timeless element in the art of 'well building'. I consider that what he strove for with tremendous courage, tenacity, humour and integrity, was the essence of an architecture that serves the human spirit and its relationship to a higher reality. These elusive qualities have to be striven for, especially in our time, when mankind, more than ever in the past, is in danger of becoming a willing slave of the machine. To quote Campbell, "There is a difference between a machine and a building; a building is not an appliance or a mobilisation. The building as architecture is born out of the heart of man; permanent consort to the ground, comrade to the trees, true reflection of man in the realm of his spirit."

> SPACE is the vehicle of architecture.
> ORDER is needed to enclose space for human purposes.
> ORDER is expressed by CONTRAST.
> CONTRAST is expressed in three dimensions by CONSTRUCTION.
> CONSTRUCTION depends on the use of TOOLS.
> TOOLS are directed by the human spirit through the hand with LABOUR.
> LABOUR is directed by WORKING DRAWINGS.

I find these concepts are embodied in Campbell's architecture in the following ways.

SPACE   to emphasise "The Within" or "Consecrated Space" there should be a *quality* of light rather than a *quantity* of light in order to make the space plastic. "Do not make too many or too large openings, 'a view' to release you from what you have made. Peer out if you must, but only to see that The Dragon is not coming up your path!"

ORDER   so that the part and the whole can be mutually supporting, a cubic unit of measure, preferably an odd number, related to the building units, is useful. Roof pitches should be uniform and there should be a separate roof for each major cell or group of cells.

CONTRAST   is obtained by balancing opposites, dark and light, high and low, plain and intricate.

CONSTRUCTION   should be practical and easily understood by the Workmen and based on the Architect's working knowledge of materials and their nature.

TOOLS   Architects can only benefit from practical experience in the workshops or on the building site.

WORKING DRAWINGS   should be clear and aimed at providing the information needed by the Workman on the site.

LABOUR   If the Architect can regard himself as another *Tradesman,* he can easily relate to those he relies on to give form to his ideas. The Workman needs a proper training to show him what he is about. Campbell urged his men to dress like builders, rather than like out of work clerks!

Illustrated letter from John Campbell to his wife Frances, quoting "Ah! Sunflower" by William Blake

JOHN CAMPBELL – ARCHITECT FOR OUR TIME

Alan Powers

ON HIS VISIT TO BIRCHENS SPRING, Christopher Hussey wrote that "Mr Campbell was a star that had not previously swum into my ken and, judging from the bold, unfamiliar design, he was a major planet." Campbell's historical identity has not been helped by the existence of three architects called John Campbell whose careers overlapped in time. To add to the confusion, two of them were called John Archibald Campbell; the subject of this book and the important Glasgow architect (1859-1909) who was in partnership with J. J. Burnet between 1886 and 1897. Ulrich Thieme's *Allgemeines Lexikon der bildenden Künstler* (Leipzig 1911) actually conflates these two in one entry. A third John Campbell (1857-1942) was a Glasgow-born architect practising in New Zealand where he designed many public buildings. None of these Campbells was related.

In addition, Campbell's most accessible works which date from the 1930s, fit uneasily in the stylistic categories established for the period. This may, however, be a useful way of understanding his present significance, because the categories "Modern" and "Traditional" are still unhelpfully seen in dualistic and irreconcilable opposition today.

The "Modern House" of the 1930s can conveniently be identified with the flat roof, or at least with anything but the equal pitched-roof, that most functional of forms. There is a succession of architects in the 1950s and 60s, such as Peter Aldington and Robert Maguire, who managed to combine elements of modern and traditional architecture without compromise, but sincere and effective attempts to bridge this gap have been rare.

Controversy has continued during the last thirty years about the true relationship between Arts and Crafts and Modernism. There was more Arts and Crafts ideology underlying the Modern Movement, in all countries, than we have generally been led to believe, but the imagery of Modern buildings was deliberately very different from these antecedents, to the extent that older Arts and Crafts architects in England like W. R. Lethaby and C.F. A. Voysey repudiated any association with the Modernism of the 1920s. The text of *The Modern House in England* (1937), by F. R. S. Yorke even opens with a two-page quotation from Lethaby (1856-1932), written in 1917, beginning thus:

"Our aim should be to develop a fine tradition of living in houses. It is a matter for experiment, like flying. We should seek to improve in detail point by point. There are enough sketch designs; now we want solids. Exquisite living on a small scale is the ideal. 'House-like' should express as much as 'ship-shape.'"

Five years after his death, Lethaby was in no position to protest at this appropriation. What his text seems to describe, however, is something very like Campbell's experiment in "exquisite living on a small scale" at Chapel Point which was nearing completion at the time that Yorke's book was published.

Campbell's views are quoted in Christopher Hussey's admiring articles on Chapel Point,

"The sterile style-cults (whether ancient or modern) are the result of looking at history pragmatically.

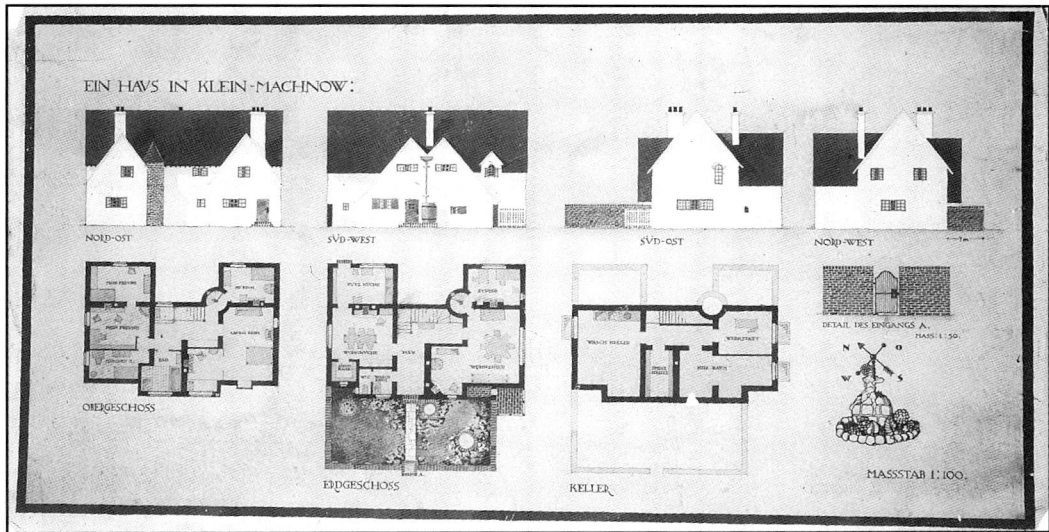

Design for own house in Klein Machnow, Berlin, 1909

It must be read as flowing like a never-ending story, not as a document. ... The present rationalistic reaction to the frivolity of the stylists is healthy, but seeks complete independence from tradition, forgetting that it was just the lack of traditional continuity and a true reading of history that has brought the stylists themselves into ill repute. After the reaction has exhausted itself, and if we are to revive from the weariness of our disillusionment, a bridge must be built for the perilous crossing from the past to the future."

While Lethaby, in despair at the failure to produce a historically-rooted Modern architecture in the first part of the century, turned his attention to other matters, Campbell tried primarily through building to resolve the problems of bridging from the past. Although he designed other types of building, the house, with which he formed his reputation in Germany, became his theme. In his subtle and thorough analysis of *The English House*, 1904 Herman Muthesius recognised the moral qualities that made Arts and Crafts more valuable than *Jugendstil*, which at the time represented modernity: "Everything breathes simplicity, homeliness and rural freshness, occasionally indeed verging on the vernacular ... instead of a sham modernity expressing itself extravagantly in whimsical artificiality we find purely functional, unaffected design that many may already regard as more modern than all the fantastic excesses of a so-called modern style."

The problem was hardly solved by the Modernism of the 1920s, as we begin to understand better in hearing an increasing number of dissenting voices within Modernism begin to emerge, and in witnessing the well-packaged concept of the "International Style" coming undone. Campbell occupies a place in this process by virtue of the quality of his best work, which has appealed to many at first sight of photographs while the personal story behind it has remained unknown. His experience in Germany gave him a dimension that English architects largely lacked, for he moved in circles where artistic and philosophical ideas were discussed hard and long. Reading and thinking undoubtedly supported his work, and the list of books which he recommended to his pupils at Blundell's School support his belief in the necessity of crossing Western civilisation with Eastern and transcending a materialist world view. ★

Re-engagement with these deeper ideas rather than historical curiosity justifies the re-examination of Campbell's work. His self-criticism helps in understanding the difficulty of the task he undertook in his bridge-building and, by extension, the relative simplicity of plunging into the mainstream of Modernism. Campbell seems to have hoped continually that Modern architects would address the same problems as he did, and perhaps find better solutions to them. He acknowledged the danger of nostalgia, writing of Chapel Point, "the houses are not clear and clean enough. I regret the element of ye oldeness clinging to them."

This is not the same, however, as the qualities of softness and sweetness which Campbell learnt to appreciate in Bavaria where Northern and Southern civilisations merge, and which were manifested in his work, acutely at times in small details and always flowing through the whole building. These qualities Modernism feared as destructive to its identity and Post-Modernism kept at bay with irony. As a way of rehearnessing the moral qualities of traditional architecture to the service of society, academic classicism has often forgotten this important lubricant. Campbell had interesting views on classicism which he did not oppose and indeed believed to be the underlying principle of all architecture, but, as recounted by Christopher Hussey in 1938, he believed that "Classicism has not necessarily anything to do with the Orders. Rightly understood, it is the corpus of the humanist theory and practice of building, enriched by three thousand years of experience; while craftsmanship is its practical corollary for the handling of materials."

Campbell lightened the lumpish tendency of later Arts and Crafts architecture without floating off into fantasy like Clough Williams-Ellis. Holding this balance was at the centre of his achievement and resulted from his development of design principles based on broader concerns. Like Voysey, he universalised regional

★ *Caravan Cities,* M. Rostovzeff
The Lord of Arabia (Ibn Saud), H. C. Armstrong.
The Study of History, A. J. Toynbee
The Decline of the West, Oswald Spengler
The Meaning of History, Berdaieff
Any literature on the '*Familia Columbia*'
The Columban Church, J. A. Duke
Christianity in Celtic Lands, Gougand
Decline and Fall, Gibbon
Petra et la Nabatene, A Kamerer

Palmyra: Eine historische-klimatische studie
The Rise and Progress of the Arts and Sciences, David Hume
Irish Monasticism: Origins and Early Developments, J. Ryan
Les Ruines: ou méditation sur les révolutions des empires,
Comte de C. F. Volney
Essai sur l'histoire politique et économique de Palmyre, Fevrier
The Rise and Decline of Civilisation, Albert Schweitzer
La poésie des races celtiques, Renan
Life of St Patrick, Bury
The Crisis of the Modern World, René Guénon.

style rather than seeking to reproduce its specifics and used white-painted brick and Delabole slates in Buckinghamshire, instead of the local brick and tile. If one searches for a comparison to Campbell's houses, one might find it in Herbert Luck North (1871-1941) of Llanfairfechan, who covered a Welsh hillside with steep-gabled white houses as Campbell wished to populate Chapel Point. North tended to Gothic, but Campbell's round arches look to the Mediterranean, qualified by his principle that "a design should depart from, by simplifying, the classic type in proportion to the distance of the site from the locality of the fountain heads" (i.e. Greece and Rome).

Campbell almost missed his vocation as a teacher, deprived of his first academic appointment in Munich by the First World War and finding it by chance only towards the end of his life, as described here by Ronald Leask, and there are few architects of his generation whose work offers such clear and comprehensible lessons. He displayed great skill in relating plan and elevation to create varied and rounded buildings, even on a small scale. The mediaeval idea of having a roof to every room (or stack of rooms) was productive in opening his buildings to light and making the simplest plans into satisfying compositions.

Simple modules control Campbell's plans, seven foot at Birchens Spring and ten foot at Chapel Point. These seem to provide the satisfying quality of underlying structure.

As traditional building craft came increasingly under threat during the Second World War, Campbell understood its value more urgently and was moved to make his major public statement in writing at length to the *Builder* about the proposed government sponsorship of pre-fabricated houses. His argument, as he summarised it, was "both technical and spiritual". Campbell was quite prepared to blame the traditional building trades for their failure to compete with modern methods, but believed they only lacked proper organisation to overcome this. Chapel Point offered the evidence that workmen could raise their level of skill when suitably challenged, and Campbell followed the Arts and Crafts aim of contributing to the well-being of the worker. He also saw the spirit in which the future occupiers of houses could become involved in the excitement of house-building, not necessarily as participants but in putting up with short-term hardship for a better end-result.

Campbell was far from unique in his relish of nature and the outdoors, but the alliance of nature and the man-made in his work is achieved in a way that preserves the integrity of both, creating identity for the building by processes analogous to natural growth but sufficiently abstracted from it to prevent the dissolution of architectural form. Thus the Chapel Point houses enhance their setting like the best vernacular buildings.

Campbell absorbed the same German philosophical background that informs Martin Heidegger's essay "Building, Dwelling, Thinking", 1951, a reflection on the essence of Space, Place and Being in their contribution to architecture's interpretation of the meaning of life. Heidegger's essay has been rediscovered as a major text for architecture in recent years and Campbell's buildings can be understood as an exploration of the same ideas. Fifty years after his death, Campbell is a more contemporary figure than anyone during the intervening years might have supposed.

JOHN CAMPBELL – A BIOGRAPHICAL CHRONOLOGY

Based on chronology by the author of the unpublished biography of Campbell, with additional information by Alan Powers. Executed works in bold, unexecuted projects in bold italic. Some dates conjectural.

1878 Born in Wolverhampton, 3 May. Home under a currant bush.

1882 Goes to Hunter's School. Goes in a paddle steamer. Converts pig-sty into a home.

1885 Goes to St Peter's School. Meets elderly recluse. Converts upper floor of stable into a home. Keeps stray dog.

1890 Evening classes at Wolverhampton School of Art.

1893 Leaves St Peter's School. Continues evening classes at the School of Art. Joins the firm of Bayliss, Jones & Bayliss, ironfounders and structural engineers.

1895 Gains Art Master's Certificate. Meets French-Welshman. Leaves Bayliss, Jones & Bayliss in order to teach at the School of Art.

1897 Given special scholarship for full-time study at Wolverhampton School of Art.

Sketchbook drawings of Mackintosh-style decoration

1898 Resigns scholarship and goes to London. Meets dissolute artist in doss-houses. Joins Waring & Gillow, Oxford Street as draughtsman and designer under Frank Murray, chief designer.

1899 Personal assistant to Frank Murray.

1900 Representative of Waring & Gillow at the Paris International Exhibition and meets German designers represented in the exhibition.

1902 Chance meeting in London with Heinrich Pössenbacher, son of Munich interior decorator Anton Pössenbacher. Travels with him for holiday in Munich and decides to remain when offered post of chief designer by Pössenbacher. Mr Kinloch comes out from England to assist him. First visit to Italy, including Vicenza, Florence and Rome. At Ravenna he decides to become an architect. Leaves Pössenbacher and briefly opens an office in Dresden.

Campbell in the offices of Campbell & Pullich, Berlin c.1908

1905 Establishes architectural practice in Berlin with Otto Pullich, chemist and philosopher. Assisted by Mr Kinloch and Eduard Pfeiffer.

1908 Marriage to Laura Gafner.

Herren-Schneiderei "Jockey Club": workroom

Herren-Schneiderei "Jockey Club", Berlin
(*Deutsche Kunst und Dekoration* XXI, 1908, pp.143-6)
Kasino (Small House) at Rombacher
Hüttenwerk, Berlin
(*Deutsche Kunst und Dekoration* XXI, 1908, pp.147-55)

Richard Schimmelpfeng House

Richard Schimmelpfeng House,
Katherinenstrasse, Zehlendorf, Berlin 1908
(*Berliner Architekturwelt*, XI, 1908-09, pp.263-68;
Berlin und Seine Bauten IVC, Berlin 1976, p.109)
First G. Schickendanz House,
19 Klopstockstrasse, Zehlendorf, Berlin 1908-
1909 (*Innen-Dekoration* XX, 1909, pp.46-53)

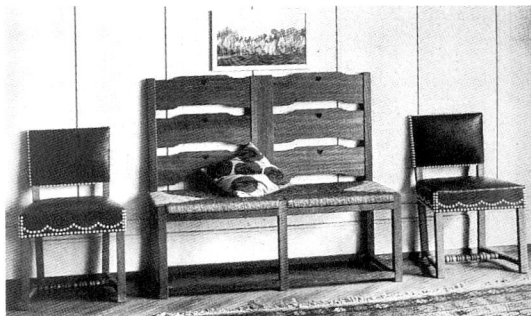

Campbell & Pullich, furniture and interiors

1909 Accidental death of Otto Pullich.
Firm of Campbell & Pullich goes bankrupt.
Campbell returns to Munich with Mr Kinloch.
With his friend Kronsbein rents house in village
of Irschenhausen, Iserthal, used for parties and
mountain excursions. Balloon trip, landing in
Russia. Other European travels. Takes house in
Werneckstrasse, Munich, with housekeeper Frau
Lechardt.
25 Heilmanstrasse, Munich (with Richard
Drach) (information from Bayerische Landesamt
für Denkmalpflege)

1910 Delegate to International Town Planning
Conference organised by RIBA, London.

Second Schickendanz House

Second Schickendanz House,
17 Klopstockstrasse, Zehlendorf, Berlin
1910-11 (*Innen-Dekoration* XXI, 1910, pp.46-53;
Berliner Architekturwelt, XVI, 1913-14, pp.162-5)
29 Heilmannstrasse, Munich Extensions and
enlargements to villa of 1901 by Max Littmann

(information from Bayerische Landesamt für
Denkmalpflege)
Haus Oberhummer, Ludwigshöhe, Munich
(*Innen-Dekoration* XXII, 1911, pp. 23-;
Innen-Dekoration XXVI, 1915, pp.365-71)
Haus W. Polich, Leipzig, interiors (*Innen-Dekoration*
XXII, 1911,)
**House in grounds of Dr Bieling's Sanatorium,
Friedrichroda**
(*Innen-Dekoration* XXII, 1911, January)

Haus Oberhummer

Odeon-Kasino, Wittelsbacher Platz, Munich (interiors), including reconstruction of Pössenbacher showroom. (*Innen-Dekoration*, 1912, pp.28–29, *Deutsche Kunst und Dekoration*, XXIX, 1911–12, pp.312–22)

Odeon Kasino, 1912

(with Richard Drach) **Landhaus Bauer, Feldafing, Munich** (*Innen-Dekoration* XXV, 1914, January, pp.2–18; *Studio Yearbook of Decorative Art*, 1924, p.61)

Grand Hotel Continental, Munich (*Innen-Dekoration* XXII, 1911, pp.2–14; XXIV, 1913, pp.2–30)

1914 Appointed Regius Professor of Architecture at Kunstgewerbeschüle, Munich on 16 July. At the outbreak of war with Britain on 4 August Campbell is stripped of his Professorship and interned in Ruhleben Civilian Prisoner–of–War Camp, Berlin.

Kurhotel, St Petersburg. Alterations to rooms (reference in unpublished biography)

1918 Repatriated in August, prior to Armistice in November. His wife Laura joins him in London in December.

Grand Hotel Continental, Munich, 1912

1919 Moves to Glastonbury and works with architect-antiquarian Frederick Bligh Bond in the excavation of Glastonbury Abbey, becoming his partner. Meets Thomas Falconer.

Design for War Memorial at Albrighton, Shropshire (*Studio* 1925)

Crediton War Memorial, Devon

1920 January, joins Falconer's practice, living at Nailsworth. The Hon. Mark Kearley, a fellow-inmate at Ruhleben, joins as assistant.

1921 Partnership of Falconer, Baker and Campbell, Amberley, Glos. Campbell acts as chief design partner.
Picket House, Avening, Gloucestershire
(*Studio Yearbook of Decorative Art*, 1923, pp.20,23; 1924, p.59: *Baukunst* 1928)
Great Rissington Manor, Gloucestershire
Extensions, interiors and garden layout for Major W. J. P. Marling (*Studio Yearbook of Decorative Art*, 1924, pp.58, 60; *Studio* 1925, *Baukunst* 1928)
Interiors for Maggs Bros Bookshop, 34 Conduit Street, London W1
(*Studio Yearbook of Decorative Art*, 1924, p.60; *Baukunst* 1928)
Bear Hotel, Rodborough Common, Gloucestershire extensions for Major H. Napier Rowlatt (*Studio* 1925)

1922 Opens branch office of Falconer, Baker and Campbell in London at 12 Buckingham St., then at 17 Soho Square, with Mark Kearley.
Friendship with Serbian philosopher Metrinovic.
Project for a concrete church (Studio 1925)
Project for Masonic Hall, Stroud (Studio 1925)
Project for Catholic Church at Haywards Heath (Baukunst 1928)
Projects for regional studios for BBC c.1928
Landhaus Heinrich Mendelsohn, Am Schwemmhorn, Kladow, Berlin, 1925-27

1928 Divorce from Laura. Dissolution of Falconer, Baker and Campbell.

1929 Sets up architectural practice in Berlin at beginning of year, chief assistant Karl Hirschbold, formerly chief assistant to Eduard Pfeiffer who died in the same year.
Completion of Bussehaus by Pfeiffer
Completion of Lettre House by Pfeiffer
Golfhaus, Nedlitz
Shop for Emil Lettre, Goldsmith, Unter den

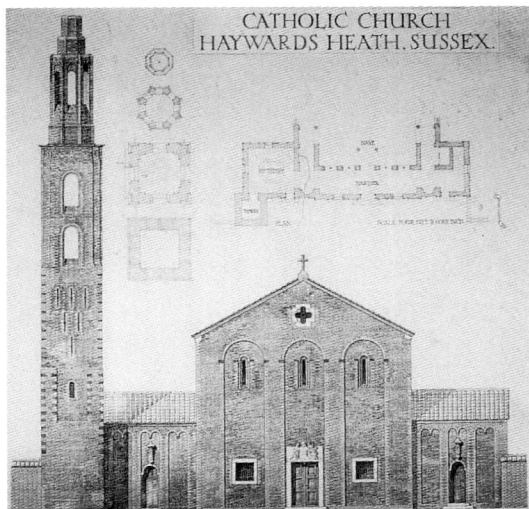

Project for Catholic Church, Haywards Heath, c.1928

House for Baroness Rothschild, c.1931

Linden
Project for house for Baroness Rothschild, Wannsee
(completed to one storey)
**Permanent exhibition of room settings
demonstrating the history of English
architecture, Wertheimer's Store, Berlin**

1930 June. Marries Frances Dagley, cabinet-maker and
furniture designer. Journey to Paris, Barcelona
and Majorca. Lives in Regentenstrasse 12, Berlin
**Alterations to Waldsanatorium, Arosa,
Switzerland**

1931 24 July. Birth of son, Colin. October, leaves
Berlin and returns to England.

1932 January. Discovers Chapel Point, Mevagissey,
Cornwall. Submission of scheme for 20 houses
at Chapel Point submitted to St Austell Rural
District Council.
First temporary wooden house, Chapel Point
Project for cinema at Teignmouth

1933 Birchens Spring, Beaconsfield finished early
1934. (*Country Life*, January 29, 1938, pp.114-8;
February 5, pp.140-4)

1935 *Project for Chiswick Mall Riverside Flats,
for H. Mendelsohn*
Chapel Point House, Mevagissey
First temporary house demolished.

1936 25 Feb Detailed plans for a fourth house at
Chapel Point, passed by St. Austell R.D.C.

1937 **Gate House, Chapel Point**, completed.
(Three Chapel Point houses illustrated in
Country Life, October 19, 1945, pp.684-7;
October 26, pp.728-31)
*Project for Marine Drive, Rottingdean
for H Mendelsohn*

1938 **Point Head Cottage, Chapel Point**, completed.
10 acres of the option on the land at Chapel
Point purchased.
Pentyr, Helford, Helston, Cornwall

1939 3 September Outbreak of war.

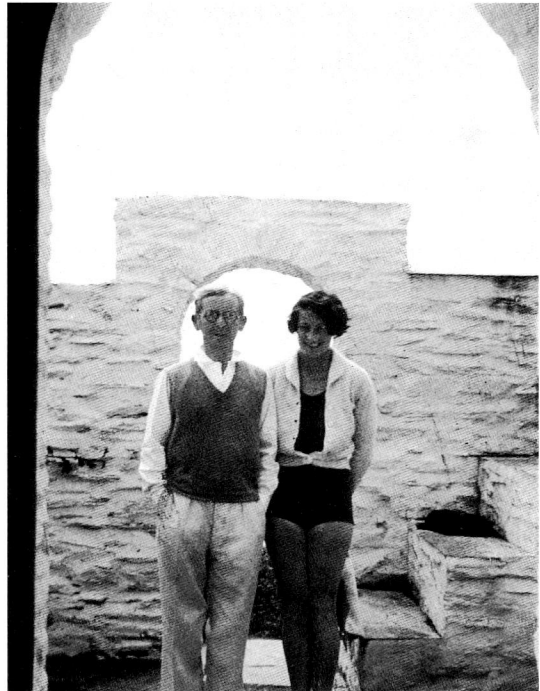

John and Frances Campbell at Chapel Point

1940 Frances and Colin Campbell leave Chapel Point
House. John Campbell's first eye operation,
Autumn.

1941 April. An architect to the Ministry of Aircraft
Production in London.

1942 May. Meeting with the Rev Neville Gorton,
Headmaster of Blundell's School, Tiverton
(later Bishop of Coventry). Goes to teach at
Blundell's. Second eye operation in December.

1943 March. Third eye operation. Chapel Point House
sold. November resigns from staff of Blundell's
School following change of Headmaster.

Building Chapel Point

1944 April. Leaves Blundell's School and goes to work in Hoxton, London with Walter Douglas and Ronald Leask. Begins work on alterations and additions to Holy Trinity Girls' and Boys' Club, Shepherdess Walk. Campbell's letter questioning pre-fabricated houses published in *Builder*, September 15, pp.214-5.

Leaves London and returns to Chapel Point, building **Second temporary wooden home, "The Ark", at Roward's Quay, Chapel Point**, completed in October.

1945 January. Returns to London and opens architectural office at 189 Brompton Road.

Project for houses on Island of Gigha, Strathclyde, for Colonel Horlick

Projects for houses in Cornwall, Devon and elsewhere

Project for rebuilding after bomb damage of All Saints, Chilvers Coton, Warwickshire

1946 Ronald Leask joins Campbell in his office as assistant, following service in Royal Marines.

House at Mawnan Smith for Mr Clayton

1947 May. Model of proposed Chapel Point development exhibited at Royal Academy Summer Exhibition (in *Architecture Illustrated*, Nov 1947, *Revue Moderne des Arts*). Campbell proposed as candidate for Associateship of the RA by E. Vincent Harris.

Project for House in Kenya for Capt. L. N. Hope (Drawings exhibited Royal Academy, 1948, *Architecture Illustrated*, Oct 1948)

12 June Plans for fourth house at Chapel Point, previously passed by St Austell RDC on 25 February 1936 resubmitted and rejected. Preparation of appeal. Camping holiday with wife and son at Chapel Point.

19 August Death of John Campbell

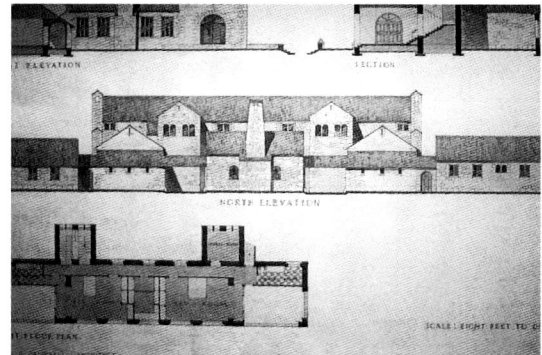

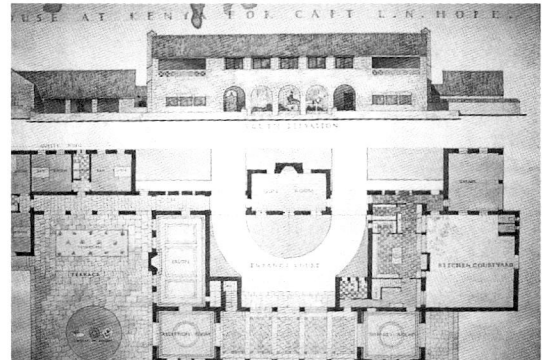

House in Kenya for Captain Hope

The following buildings by Campbell in England are listed Grade II :

Bear Hotel, Rodborough Common

Great Rissington Manor

Birchens Spring (now Drummer's Yard)

Gate House, Chapel Point House and Point Head Cottage

BOOKS

Cane, Percy S., *Modern Gardens British and Foreign*, London, The Studio, 1926-7 (Great Rissington Manor)

Architecture Club, *Recent English Architecture*, London, Country Life Ltd 1947 (House at Mevagissey)

Hadfield, Miles, *The Art of the Garden*, London, Studio Vista, 1965, p.146 (Great Rissington Manor)

Kornwolf, James D., *M. H. Baillie Scott and the Arts and Crafts Movement, Pioneers of Modern Design*, Baltimore and London, Johns Hopkins Press, 1972, pp.338-9 (house designs 1908)

PERIODICALS

Studio, XXXV, 1905, pp.254-8, "Studio-Talk: Munich"

Innen-Dekoration, XVII, 1906, January, Adolf Vogt, "Ein Neues Atelier für Wohnungs-Kunst", pp.1-16

Deutsche Kunst und Dekoration, XXI (October 1907-March 1908), pp.126-38 & 139-58, "Campbell & Pullich, Berlin" projects: Herren-Schneiderei Jockey-Club, Berlin; Kasino der Rombacher Hüttenwerke)

Deutsche Kunst und Dekoration, XXII (April - September 1908), pp.241-54, 'Das Landhaus Schimmelpfeng in Zehlendorf' by Campbell and Pullich (text by Alfred Vogt)

Innen-Dekoration, XIX, June 1908, pp.183-192 "Neue Arbeiten von Campbell & Pullich"

Berliner Architekturwelt, XI, 1908-09, pp.263-68 (Landhaus Schimmelpfeng, Katharinenstrasse, Zehlendorf, Berlin)

Innen-Dekoration, XX, 1909, pp.16-33, Max Osborn, "Campbell & Pullich–Berlin"; 429-32

Innen-Dekoration, XXI, 1910, pp.46-53, (Second Haus Schickendanz, Berlin)

Innen-Dekoration, XXII, 1911, pp.1-38 (Hotel Continental, Munich, interiors Landhaus Oberhummer, Munich)

Innen-Dekoration, XXIII, 1912,

Deutsche Kunst und Dekoration, XXVII, 1910-11, pp.374-81 Hotel Continental, Munich

Innen-Dekoration, XXII, 1911, January, pp.1-38, "Neue Arbeiten von Ino A. Campbell in München" by Fritz von Ostini (Landhaus Bauer, Feldafing with Richard Drach)

Deutsche Kunst und Dekoration, XXIX, 1911-12, pp.312-22, Odeon-Kasino, Munich

Innen-Dekoration, XXIII, 1912, January Odeons-Kasino, Munich, pp.28-29, Wilhelm Michel, "Neue Arbeiten von Ino A. Campbell". (Haus Hupfeld, Leipzig–interiors)

Innen-Dekoration, XXIV, 1913, January, pp.2-30 (Grand Hotel Continental, Munich)

Berliner Architekturwelt, XVI, 1913-14, pp.162-5 (Landhaus Schinkendanz, Klopstockstrasse)

Innen-Dekoration, XXV, 1914, January, pp.2-18 (Grand Hotel Continental, Munich)

Innen-Dekoration, XXVI, 1915, June, pp.365-71 (Landhaus Oberhummer, Prinz-Ludwigshohe, Munich, house and garden)

Studio Yearbook of Decorative Art, 1923, pp.20-23, "Sunk Garden in the Cotswold district, with thatched garden room and terrace" (Picket House, Avening)

Studio Yearbook of Decorative Art, 1924, pp.28, 58-61 (Great Rissington Manor, exteriors and interiors, interiors of House in South Cotswolds, Library at 34 Conduit Street, House on Lake Starnberg, Bavaria)

Studio, 1925, pp.25-27, 86-89, "The Work of Messrs. Falconer, Baker and Campbell" by S[hirley] B. W[ainwright] (Masonic Hall, Stroud project, Figure for Albrighton War Memorial, Concrete Church project, Great Rissington Manor, Rathaus project)

Baukunst, Munich VI, June 1928, pp.148-172, "John A. Campbell in England in Gemeinschaft mit Thos. Falconer und Harold Baker" by R[udolf] P[fister]. (Haus Bauer, Feldafing, The Bear Inn Hotel, Rodborough Common, Maggs's Bookshop interiors, Great Rissington Manor Gardens)

Studio Yearbook of Decorative Art, 1930, p.100 (Wardrobe in oregon pine, designed by John Campbell, made in workshop of Frances Dagley, Harrow. Other examples of Frances Dagley's designs are on pp.80, 100)

Country Life, January 29, 1938, pp.114-8; February 5, pp.140-4. "Birchens Spring, Beaconsfield" by Christopher Hussey

Builder, September 15, 1944, pp.214-15 Letter "The Portal Houses, principles involved"

Country Life, October 19, 1945, pp.684-7; October 26, pp.728-31, "Houses at Chapel Point, Mevagissey, Cornwall" by Christopher Hussey

Builder, September 26, 1947, p.352 obituary

Architecture Illustrated, November 1947 (model of Chapel Point development)

Art et Industrie, X, 1948, pp.48-50 "La Pierre et l'ardoise sont également des matériaux préfabriqués, disait John Campbell, l'architecte de Chapel-Point en Cornouailles" by Christopher Hussey

Architecture Illustrated, October, 1948 (model of house in Kenya)

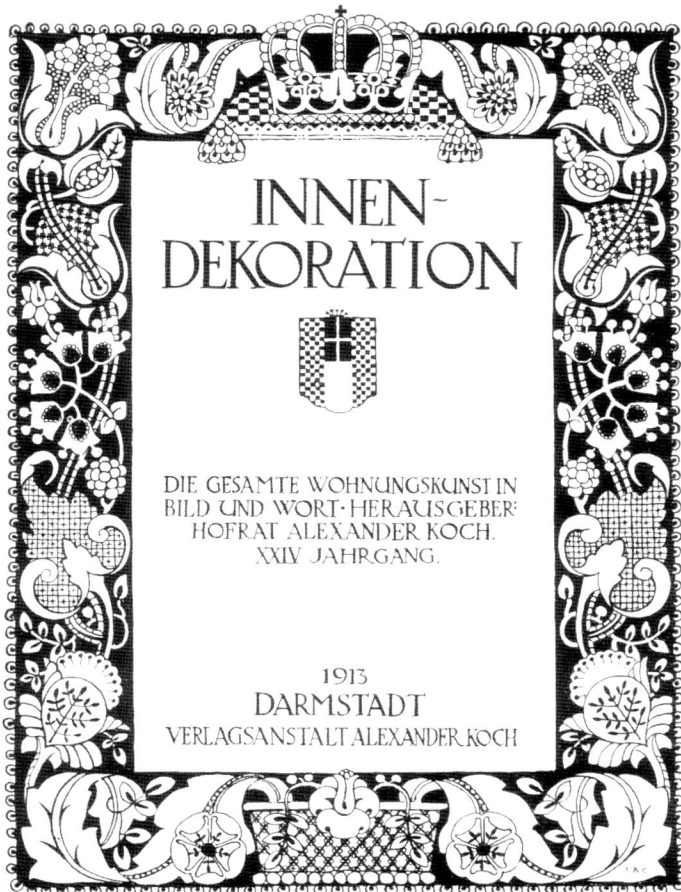

Innen Dekoration, decorative title page by John Campbell, c.1910

Chapel Point House, 1935, John Campbell's living room

Extracts from "Just a talk: a lecture to academic travellers met at an inn", given by John Campbell at Blundell's School, c.1943. Complete text in unpublished biography.

ARCHITECTURE IS MAN'S WORK WHEN HE MAKES CONSECRATED SPACE

S TANDARDISED LEARNING HAS confused architecture with archaeology or with chaos, but it is neither of these things. It is, and always has been, the work of adoration and the solving of ever new building problems with courage, imagination and integrity. It is a noble response to high necessity through good craftsmanship, unity and clarity. It is the thought of to-day, wrought with eagerness and care.

We should not bother our heads about good or bad 'taste' when considering an object. The man of 'taste' observes form, proportion and detail; the more he absorbs the more he thinks he knows. But these things are ever-changing effects of a cause which is vital and eternal. Joy and fervour, sweetness and gaiety, rapture and ecstasy: these are the stuff from which beauty is made. Therefore we should look for other qualities in an object than that of 'taste'. Bravery, tenderness and robustness should delight us, and we should have the heart to forgive a stammering if we can discern a wistful yearning for expression. To aim consciously at achieving 'style' is to follow a will o' the wisp, for the pursuit of 'style' is like the pursuit of happiness: both must necessarily lead to disappointment and failure. Both are alike by-products, and the quality of the ideal pursued. No man can form a thing to 'look well.' Good form is not 'good form' nor any shape, but, like well-doing, is a thing of the spirit.

He who would aim at 'style' is he who would gild the lily instead of watering it. Style is a quality of the flower of things, only to be gained by root-culture. Style is the art of architecture, so it cannot be an aim. If we start aright with first principles, it may be the result.

So architecture cannot be any 'style' or any 'mode.' However much the outward garment of architecture changes, and it is always changing with the changing conditions of life, there are certain elements that remain constant at all times and in all places. When looking back at past achievement it is for these universal laws and principles that we must look. We have to look within all great buildings of the past for such working of these principles as made them new in the order of their day. As a matter of course, the particular forms and details appropriate to them must become eccentricities to us – fatal should we try to copy them.

We must look for the beauty which lies inherent in the structure, common to all periods yet independent of the form of expression of any period. Architecture was never old and will be ever new because the Law that runs through it was old before the heavens and the earth were made. It cannot be considered in terms of styles or periods but only in terms of something vitally important to this present and belonging to this present.

I wish all architects were practical builders. The trouble with architects is that they often regard themselves as gentlemen and not as tradesmen, and especially is this so to-day when it is the architectural colleges that produce them.

If we are to be saved to-day the local and temporary things that lie deep in the essence of western civilisation must and should be broadened to have world wide validity.

Modern man is becoming increasingly aware of

his hopeless position: there are clear signs of it. For half a century at least there have been revolts against it. One of the first rebels was Mackintosh of Glasgow. A little later came the French, Darmstadt and Vienna movements. We must not forget the Pre-Raphaelite movement, or William Morris, the most honourable of the lot. But all these were 'art' movements, reactions or revivals within the accepted historic picture, each being a little Renaissance on its own which came like the big one, got sick when young and died, proving frailer than the big brother who survived them and can still be seen, grey haired, with crutch but with well tailored coat, in our streets. These frail but valiant movements died but were not forgotten. They did not live in vain, for from their ashes rose a healthier, robuster school of 'modernists'. For those who had been so long frequenting graveyards it was good to hear their lusty voices cry out: 'To Hell with everything. To Hell with culture. To Hell with wood – we'll cut it up into leaves as thin as paper, we'll steam and twist out

Chapel Point House: aerial perspective

all its nature to our wills. We're honest men who see things as they are. We'll chromium plate all iron to hide the beastly stuff. To Hell with tradition!'

We are not offended at these words of the 'modernists' for we have been accustomed in these latter days to a tradition of bad habits. But, when they cry: 'To Hell with History!' then we see with consternation that they are but another movement within the framework of the Greek-Medieval-Renaissance-Modern picture of history, destined to play its allotted part and then pass into decline with the rest.

It would now be appropriate to support my words with pictures. I will divide them into two groups. The first:
Greek-Medieval-Renaissance-Modern.
The second:
Arabian-Byzantine-Romanesque-Modern.

Group 1: A Greek Temple
A Gothic Cathedral
A Renaissance Palace
A Modern Utility Building

Group 2 An Arabian Building
A Byzantine Church
A Romanesque Church
A Modern Utility Building

Of course, we can look at the first three pictures of buildings in each group with justified awe and astonishment as works of art. But I am inviting you to look at them more coldly, and for a different purpose. What you see can confirm or refute my thesis.

In the first group I see buildings of great attainment, impenetrably bounded from each other and from us. Great works they are, living in the isolation of their own time and place, entirely expressing the local moment, only understandable and useful to it.

The buildings of the second group affect me very differently. They all seem strangely related to each other, and to us. I feel some universal, timeless truth pervading them.

There are certain characteristics (forms) of wide-ranging validity which are independent of the culture and century to which they belong; but along with these, there is a quite particular necessity of form which underlies all thought as axiomatic and to which everyone is subject by virtue of belonging to one world-culture and no other. ... As in the Romanesque, so to a greater degree in the Syriac from which it sprang, there is something of the universal and eternal, expressed in direction, line, destiny; and it is this something which seems to me to appear in all the first three pictures of Group 2, and to bind them together and make them comprehensible to us. ...

The SYRIAC depicts for me:–
Algebra, astronomy, astrology, alchemy, mosaics, and arabesques. (The Early Christian Church of the Nativity at Bethlehem is built over a natural cave.)
Space covered-in. To aim, it sets a possible limit.
The tangible-intangible.
The dome soars free like the Gothic, and yet it encloses the Great Cavern.
The capture and control of space covered with gleaming ornament - ornament that is not pictorial - surface decoration.
Vaulting saturated with colour.
Column and round arch.
Tendency to fill up the surface.
Anti-plastic to the last degree and hostile to the pictorial.
It draws its endless richness over it like a web.
The world as a cavern,
Inwardness.
The spatial definitely limited.
The circle revolving upon itself.
The very presence of God.
Young and radiant religion.
Algebraic indeterminateness of number.
The domed chamber.
Gold takes the place of colour.

... It is not the mere superficial response to an eastern cult of the past that attracts us, but something very vital which meets the modern innate need. On the contrary, it is just those purely Arabian expression-forms which have been retained to which we can not respond, such as the horse-shoe arches. It is not the Arabian style of architecture which appeals to us, but the space-conceptions of the Syriac; a polaric force which the maternal west has had need of in the depths of her soul throughout history. ...

Should we be very wrong, acquainted as we are with so many other characteristics of that with which we are dealing, if we envisaged the dawn of such an architecture thus: a group of long, low buildings, all quite simple as befits the dawn of architecture, with here and there a great Hall rising slightly higher than the other buildings? It might have all been planned round a courtyard by some monk who knew his Greek geometry. The courtyard might be laid out in squares and circles, and joined to other courtyards by great semi-circular headed gateways. The feature that the foreign visitor would retain in his mind always would be the great round towers that rose from the groups of buildings. If not quite like this, I am sure it would have been something equally simple and clear in plan, expressing to an equal degree confidence and hope.

And what of the development of such an architec-

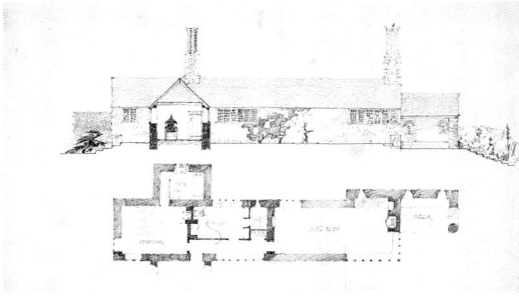

Chapel Point House: early version of design

THE PORTAL HOUSES:
PRINCIPLE INVOLVED

To the Editor of the Builder

SIR, - An emergency factory-made house has been presented to the public. It is to be a solution of the real and grave problem of the shortage of housing accommodation for the people after the war. A prototype of the house has been put up in the garden of the Tate Gallery. There can be no doubt that it shows a very intelligent and earnest, and from the technical point of view a very able, attempt to solve the problem as presented.

The proposers and their supporters offer a well-thought-out solution. No more is claimed for it than that it is immediate and temporary. In the complete and efficient way in which it is presented it is hard to criticise it. The dislike of the idea of the house that is certainly felt by a growing number of people cannot therefore be grounded in the main, on a purely practical or technical basis. If the house is vulnerable, it is not because of its virtues, which are manifest. In the completeness of its presentation

it claims to be more than temporary. It claims to be the best solution yet of all the difficulties that confront the housewife. If it is vulnerable it is because it is based upon a false principle.

The primary object of this letter is to examine the principle underlying this solution of the problem; and only in the second place to propose an alternative. This principle must be examined as objectively as possible, and if it seems to be of a disruptive nature, then it is possible that there, and not in any claims that may be made for the house by the proposers, the root of the misgiving lies.

The violent break with building tradition represented by this house can be justified in two ways only. Either the house is the only possible way of meeting the demand of the moment, or it is only a beginning, born out of the stress of the moment, of an attempt at a permanent solution of the housing problem, other than by traditional means.

The disadvantages of the emergency factory-made house, in meeting the demand of the moment are wide and varied. They must be obvious, not least to the proposers themselves. This is indeed acknowledged in the statement that the house is only an immediate and temporary solution. The only argument in its support that can here be justified is that of speed of supply and erection superior to any other kind of suitable building. Its position is unassailable if this can be conclusively proved.

The brick manufacturers and the trade of bricklaying could not, as at present constituted, deal with the problem in the traditional way. This is as certain as that the claims made for the speed of supply and erection of the factory-made house are themselves debatable. It would be necessary to face the idea of a traditional solution in an unorthodox way. There might be conscription into the trade. To a call to rebuild this battered land there are few who would not willingly respond. To train a million brick makers and bricklayers to do the sort of work required should be no harder than to train millions of unskilled men to use the exact instrument of war or to get coal from the mines. The clay for the bricks is present in almost limitless quantities, and the supply of other things necessary should not be impossible.

To face the problem in a traditional way might involve no more difficulties than to face it in the way proposed. It might require organisation. But in this mechanical age we tend to go straight to the mechanical solution, as a matter of course. It is felt that to fight against mechanisation, even when it may be stepping outside its sphere, is impossible.

But perhaps the house, like so many other articles, may be in the process of being proved suitable to mass-production in the factory, and the traditional ways of building may be outmoded or confined to a dwindling luxury trade?

Whatever the success in the application of mass-production to the fittings of a house, its structure is a thing far too intimately associated with the ground upon which it lies, and the skies above it, ever to be suited to such a method. Many of the difficulties that have confronted and will confront the proposers of the factory-made house are the results of trying to get round this truth. To try to mass-produce the structure of a house is to court, in the end, technical disaster.

Nevertheless, it is more than likely that an attempt to do so will shortly be proposed, not as a temporary immediate solution to the housing problem, but as a permanent one. In this way the great industrial interests will seek to draw the building trade, one of the noblest of the remaining English

crafts, into the factory for good. It is probable that the mass-produced house will be publicised as a structure with all the advantages of skilled planning and convenience that the ability of the age can put into it. As such, it will be suggested that it is capable of fulfilling a permanent wide need in a cheaper, quicker, fuller, if not in a better, way than the house built by traditional means.

A danger of such gravity to the whole of the

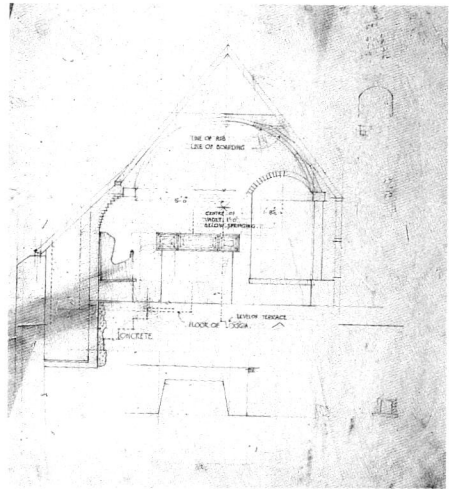

Chapel Point House: section of living room

building trade cannot be faced by saying that the trade is powerful and influential, and that it would on no account tolerate the extension of the mass-produced house beyond the sphere of the immediate and the temporary. Has any trade in the course of history ever made a stand against the encroachments of the factory with success? Even the falsity of the principle of applying these methods to building structure as a whole will not stop the attempt to impose them and gain their rewards.

Whichever way one tries to justify the break with building tradition represented by the emergency factory-made house one meets with a false principle. If it is proposed as the only possible way of meeting the demands of the moment, then those demands might be better met by traditional methods, using the same amount of ability and organisation. If it is regarded as the beginning of a permanent attempt at the solution of the housing problem, other than by traditional means, then there are those things in its nature which are bound to ensure its failure, and to prove an unjustifiable menace to the regular trade.

The emergency factory-made house seems but another outcome of that ruling idea of expediency that really controls the policy of this country to-day. As part of that idea it can only end, leaving the technical grounds out of the picture, by being proved fruitless and an illusion. It makes no claim to satisfy the deepest desires in the heart of man.

"Where there is no vision the people perish". To give them bread and the plans of Beveridge and Portal is not in the end enough. Men are not only body, requiring security and a measure of ease. They are also mind and spirit. They require continual strife and the onward press, disregarding convenience, in the quest for the truth. Any solution, whether it be for well-being of nations or for a housing problem, that takes no account of these things, is doomed to utter failure. If the people of this country were going to put away their arms when the fighting stops, and embrace a life of immediate comfort and ease, then indeed there would be much to be said for the idea of expediency. Within the lifetime of the factory-made house the things for which the war was begun would have been lost. But

the people are not wanting to do this. They seek a leader in the peace, as they have so signally found one in war. They demand to be guided to create, if necessary, with their new and permanent homes, their gardens, and a right way of learning and godly life for themselves and their families. To do this they will face any hardship, and they will have no truck with expedients, the second-rate, the temporary, or anything less than the truth. They will be prepared to go on living, if necessary, as they have gallantly lived in war, in Nissen huts or in tents, with their families or without them, until the true walls have risen for ever, the waste places are become green, and the peace is won . Do we forget the sort of people that we are now that we are in the hour of victory? Do we forget the dignity of man?

Seeing, as we must, the dangers and weaknesses that the idea of the emergency factory-made house presents, and that it is only a very small part of a wider wrongness of outlook, both technical and spiritual, we should intensify our inquiry into other possibility of meeting the situation presented to us through traditional methods, and in a lasting manner. We should look to it that we place first things first in these brave times. Only so can the soul of man be satisfied, and the future of the things for which so many have died be finally assured.

The "Portal Houses" were prefabricated single storey houses named after Lord Portal, First Commissioner of Buildings and Works in the War Cabinet. Several were built for public viewing outside the Tate Gallery in July 1944, including the ARCON Mark 4, Pressed Steel. Tarran and Uni-Seco. 41,000 ARCON houses were subsequently manufactured.

Facing: Chapel Point House, westward view through house and garden towards sea.

CAMPBELL BEGAN HIS CAREER as a designer with the furnishing and decorating firm, Waring & Gillow, "working up, with endless patience, elaborate large-sized colour perspectives for clients, of anything from a cottage dining-room to the Throne Room in the palace of an Indian prince."

The firm's style was completely eclectic, relying on a wide knowledge of "period" detail but it was an excellent training in an atmosphere where artistic talent was encouraged. The principal evidence of this period is Campbell's sketchbook, in which the earliest dated drawings are from 1900. It includes 17th century furniture, Adam and neoclassical detail and, on two pages, figures in rose garlands in the style of Margaret Macdonald Mackintosh which could have been taken from direct observation or from magazine illustrations. Waring & Gillow employed the finest craftsmen and Campbell learned much from them.

It is surprising that so few English designers

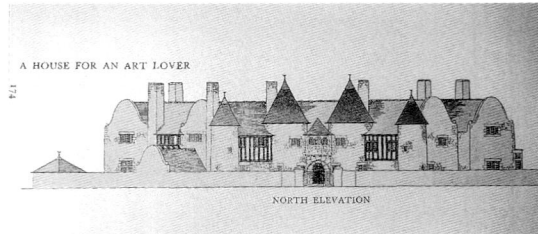

M.H. Baillie Scott, House for an art lover, 1900

went to work in Germany in the Edwardian period. Campbell indeed appears to be unique in this respect and, apart from his obvious talent, benefited from the curiosity value attached to an English designer. A high point of British influence in Germany was the award of first prize in the competition to design 'A house for an art lover' organised by the magazine *Zeitschrift für Innendekoration*, published by Alexander Koch of Darmstadt. Charles Rennie Mackintosh came second. Baillie Scott's designs continued to be published in Germany through the 1900s, although he did not build in Germany himself. Baillie Scott's influence on Campbell can be clearly seen in his earliest published designs, and in Campbell's drawing style, even before the publication of Scott's *Houses and Gardens* in 1906. It persists throughout Campbell's life, with the conical capped round towers of the 1901 design reappearing at Birchens Spring in the 1930s. Campbell's drawings of rooms, like Scott's, often show a single wing chair with a chintz loose-cover, standing forward from a deep inglenook, an invitation to enter the drawing in imagination.

Baillie Scott was a good master to follow, with a mature sense of architectural form, of furniture

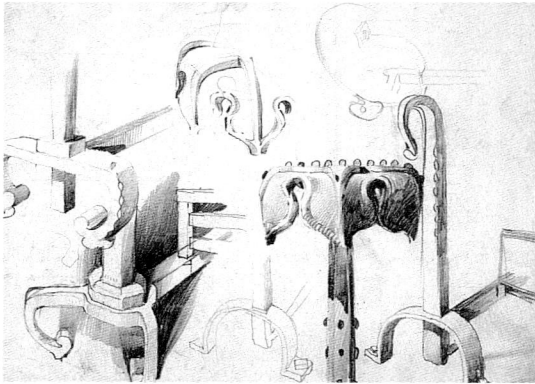

Sketch of ironwork, c.1900

Cottage design, 1909

design and interior decoration. Campbell must have responded to the purity of mass revealed in his white rendered surfaces and even carried this further. His primary architectural impulses, as he recounted them later in life, were the churches of Ravenna and London buildings seen by moonlight.

Campbell was certainly not alone in experiencing Baillie Scott's influence in Germany. During the rapid economic development of the country in the 1890s, middle-class taste favoured dark and heavy reproductions of early Renaissance style. Into this atmosphere came Jugendstil, a deliberately novel form of ornament favoured around 1900 and shown in the Paris exhibition of 1900 where Campbell had his first contact with German design. Within a few years German architects were in reaction against the preciousness and eccentricity of Jugendstil, even those who had participated in the movement, and the English influence was considered a moderating one. The Munich correspondent of the

Studio, "C.P.", wrote in 1905 that "Campbell has battled against those new 'wild' movements upon the very ground whence they sprang and secured their first foothold. By a careful study of German conditions and a realisation of the German domestic wants and needs, he has succeeded, not without struggle, in transplanting the germ of England's traditional life into the country."

While there were signs that an ornament-free, rectilinear modern architecture was beginning in Germany and Austria at this time, there was a revival of interest in the neo-classical and Biedermeier styles, manifested in buildings of around 1910 by Peter Behrens, Bruno Paul and Paul Mebes, even by Bruno Taut and Walter Gropius. Campbell was more interested in vernacular sources, even if these included a rustic classical influence. His first three years were spent working for Anton Pössenbacher of Munich whose operations were evidently similar to those of Waring & Gillow. Campbell's arrival coincided with the opening of Pössenbacher's new shop in

Sketch of interior

the centre of Munich in 1902. The firm was already 120 years old, and as a later German writer recalled, "closely connected with the Munich style of interior decoration, still dominated by the 'old German' room and exuberance of 'Art Nouveau'. In this context, Campbell's 'refreshing originality of design for furniture and interior decoration' was a great influence." The interiors of the Villa Polich at Leipzig-Gauch, published under Pössenbacher's name in *Innen-Dekoration* in December 1905 look like Campbell's work, with Arts and Crafts plaster ceilings, plain dining room panelling and a staircase with a pierced decorative balustrade and prominent newel posts. Further work in this house was published under Campbell's own name in 1911.

Campbell was already in search of a new direction by 1905, having been inspired to become an architect by his visit to Ravenna. After

Living-Hall, c. 1908

a short spell in Dresden he moved to Berlin and went into partnership with Otto Pullich, a German–American, a chemist and philosopher by training, who managed the finances leaving the design work entirely to Campbell.

The partnership was first noted in an article in *Innen-Dekoration*, the magazine which had published much English Arts and Crafts work, in January 1906. Their showroom in Dorotheen strasse gave the art-loving public "the opportunity to study English creations at close quarters – and one can see a goodly representation of England there." The article by Anton Jaumann in *Innen-Dekoration* for June 1908 spoke of the partners' attempt to find a middle way between the reproductive styles of conventional decorators and the modernism of the time:

"In activity thoroughly nourished by the past, they sought to discover through their works and through their whole activity whatever they found missing elsewhere. What this meant in this connection was a synthesis: a blending of retrospective elements, of forms and feelings which derive from tradition and of elements from their vision predicting a more refined and deepened culture of the future."

It was a moment of considerable tension in German architecture and decoration, where theoretical discussion played a much more important role than in England. After their success at the Paris Exhibition of 1900, German designers had abandoned Jugendstil (Art Nouveau) and moved in differing directions. *Sachlichkeit*, (simplification adapted for industrial production) was one course, while there was also a strong movement in favour

Lady's bedroom, Innen–Dekoration, *1909*

of drawing inspiration from folk art. The modernisers, led by Hermann Muthesius, clashed with more conservative representatives of the applied art trades in 1906 at the moment when German design was achieving a reputation all over Europe and the result in 1907 was the foundation of the *Deutsche Werkbund* as a new forum for discussion and propaganda. In returning to Munich from Berlin in 1909 Campbell was returning to the chief centre of activity, for the 1908 *Kunstgewerbe Austellung* (Applied Art Exhibition) there was recognised, particularly in France, as the peak of achievement in German design.

Campbell drew much from the Arts and Crafts and had an agency for selling William Morris fabrics, but while the movement was in decline in England he was able to give it a new lease of life in Germany. As Rudolf Pfister wrote in 1928:

"The puritan outlook of a Scottish highlander protected him from the dangers of an all-too-arty interpretation. It was not 'salons' that were designed in the Campbell studio, but rooms with a kind of monumental countrified character, full of a Nordic severity and freshness, far removed from all Gaelic over-refinement, full of quality yet without vanity."

Campbell was comparable in his range of work – furniture, interiors, domestic items – to the better-known German designers of the time such as Peter Behrens, Richard Riemerschmidt, Bruno Paul, and Heinrich Tessenow. His interior designs show a transformation at this time from the heavier style he had brought from England towards a lighter, more feminine manner. It is probably not accidental that the 1908 article illustrates such items as a "Tochter-Zimmer" with a

Design for a Rathaus.

Töchter-Zimmer, from Innen-Dekoration, *June 1908*

curtained inglenook and a cottagey living room suitable for a single lady. In this year of his own marriage he also published a bedroom with twin four-posters and explored the compositional theme of duality with a rush-seated bench in the form of two chairs joined. He was also becoming an architect at this crucial time. His surviving drawing for a house for himself and his wife is modest in scale, showing separate bedrooms and

Light fitting, c.1908

including a room for a friend, perhaps influenced by Nietzsche's insistence on the need for high thinkers to have a friend, "the cork that prevents the conversation ... from sinking to the depths." The drawings for a cottage of 1909 are in the same vein. The undated scheme for a *Rathaus* shows a different approach, betraying perhaps in its avoidance of grand composition Campbell's lack of architectural training but evidently proposing something in its place that pays more respect to the scale of old cities and turns a monumental building into a cluster of recognisable parts, as the great Munich architect-teacher Theodor Fischer achieved in the *Rathaus* project at Worms, 1905-13.

The firm of Campbell & Pullich failed financially after Pullich's accidental death in 1909 and Campbell returned to Munich, with offers of work from Pössenbacher and glad to breathe a more relaxed air. He brought with him his assistant Eduard Pfeiffer who later started his own practice in Munich and is perhaps the architect most closely allied to Campbell in style.

Campbell spent a lot of time in the mountains in a romantic retreat at Irschenhausen. From his first arrival in Germany he had a romantic attachment to German provincial architecture and a strong awareness of its division into northern and southern characteristics, writing:
"I found that south Germany is the gate to northern Italy. I went and saw unbelievable, beautiful Gothic towns in north Germany, little and not well known enough abroad. Through all these things I felt myself immeasurably enriched."

The Munich work responds to the softness of Bavaria and the classicising tendency of the south. The red white and gold interiors of the Odeon-Kasino in Munich are fit for *Der Rosenkavalier*. His work at this time was mainly concerned with interiors, including the extensive fitting out of the Hotel Continental and a number of private houses. In these a classical style is apparent, but like a few of his English contemporaries, Campbell managed an easy transition to rustic simplicity, represented in the Landhaus Bauer at Feldafing and the gardens and interiors of the Haus Oberhummer at Ludwigshohe. These later works are fuller and richer than the work of five years earlier and seem further removed from the Modernist tendency revealed in the Cologne Werkbund Exhibition of 1914, which remains for historians the principal orientation point.

Campbell undoubtedly became a significant figure in Germany during the years 1908–14, judging from the space given to his work in the magazines, *Innen-Dekoration* and *Deutsche Kunst und Dekoration*, published by Koch, the supporter of Baillie Scott and Mackintosh. For each successive year after 1908 his work filled much of the January issue of *Innen-Dekoration*, for which he also designed a decorative title page. Campbell's appointment as Professor of Architecture at the *Kunstgewerbeschule*, Munich, one of the most significant schools of design in Germany, was the recognition of his achievement, the only other significant foreigner in such a position being the Belgian Henri van der Velde at the School of Art in Weimar, later the Bauhaus.

George Schickendanz Houses, Klopstockstrasse 19, Zehlendorf, Berlin,1908-1909

Campbell's earliest architectural work is a fine and simple composition, plaster rendered and painted white, with green windows, well up to the standard of Baillie Scott. The emphasis on simple massing recalls Campbell's observations of buildings by moonlight in his early years in London, and perhaps still more the impulse he received in Ravenna which made him determined to extend his range from interior design to architecture. On that occasion, he received a revelation of the pure form of buildings, where previously he had been more concerned with decorative detail.

The description of the house given in his own words in *Innen-Dekoration* emphasises the colour of the garden planting, the decorative floor of the hallway in brick and sandstone, with ornaments and aphorisms. The newel posts of the stair are individually carved, but in strong and simple forms.

The dining room, with its very Baillie Scott-like dining alcove, is hung with William Morris fabric, and the double doors are designed to give a view through to the living room fire. The dining room sideboard, with planked doors joined by dovetails, resembles the lighter furniture of W. R. Lethaby rather than that of Baillie Scott.

Campbell wrote, "I have tried to make the house homely and comfortable without undue self-importance. I think that through simple and logical construction, through interestingly worked door and window fittings etc. the house has achieved a character, for example one sees at intervals through the building solid door frames of the same stone as that from which the house is built."

A second house for the same client was built on the adjacent plot, on the corner with Schillerstrasse. A little half-timbering appears over the entrance in the internal angle, but otherwise the exterior is very austere, with small windows in large areas of wall.

George Schickendanz Houses, Klopstockstrasse 19, Zehlendorf, Berlin, 1908-9

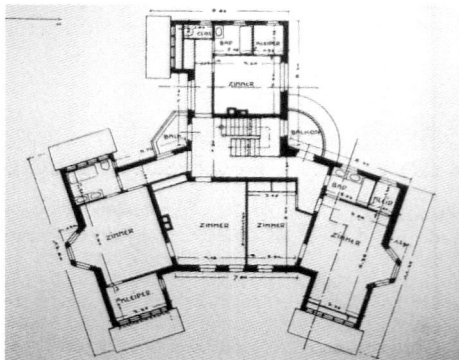

*Landhaus Bauer, Feldafing, Starnbergersee, Bavaria
(with Richard Drach), c.1912*

The plan type is the butterfly plan, a favourite
among English Arts and Crafts architects such as E.
S. Prior and Detmar Blow, who acknowledged the
influence of Ernest Gimson on the plan of his
thatched Happisburgh Manor, Norfolk. Campbell's
version has a German steep-pitched roof. A
German critic wrote: "He had come to the conclu-
sion that architecturally one must not consider walls
the frontiers, but that it must extend to all that is in
the house. He chose all the towels and sheets, even
the table mats in the Bauer Haus, and the carpets,
the knives and the forks and all of the furniture
were made by him."

Landhaus Bauer garden

Scheme for a settlement of small houses.
Records of this scheme consist only of photographs of the model. The simple houses are similar to designs by Parker & Unwin and Baillie Scott for Hampstead Garden suburb, and the layout strongly suggested the influence of the English Garden City movement, which Campbell would have seen at first hand on his return visit to London for the RIBA Town Planning Conference in 1910.

Hotel Continental, Munich, bedroom furniture

41

IN 1920 CAMPBELL JOINED the Cotswold architect Thomas Falconer and in 1921 became one of three partners in the practice of Falconer, Baker & Campbell. He had not been able to transfer any of his considerable German reputation and had to start again from scratch, but Falconer was good at getting commissions and Baker managed the business, leaving Campbell free to design. The attribution of his personal contribution to the practice is based on the works which he allowed to be published in articles in *Studio* 1925 and *Baukunst* 1928, which also correspond to the drawings and photographs which he retained.

Several important architect-craftsmen, notably Ernest and Sidney Barnsley and Ernest Gimson settled in the Cotswolds at the turn of the century, being joined by Alfred Powell, Norman Jewson and F. L. Griggs. All these figures combined architecture at some point in their career with a wider interest in the decorative arts and their social and moral importance, reflecting the ideas of John Ruskin and William Morris. They resisted the change in Edwardian architecture towards classical and Georgian styles and tended to design only buildings in the Cotswold locality where the local building traditions gave strong guidance for design. The inability of these architects to sustain their influence on native architecture even up to the time of the First World War has been seen as a failure of English architectural patronage and understanding, possibly as a result of these designers preferring to stick to old methods of construction and traditional design imagery – a by-word

for escapism in an area which economic backwardness had preserved from the ugliness of the modern world.

Campbell fitted into this company, although there is no record of personal friendships with these well-established figures. He employed the cabinet maker and joiner Peter Waals who had worked for Ernest Gimson. He wrote, "When my internment was done, I came as a European colonist to my homeland, strangely familiar but strangely distant. It was my good fortune to find my way modestly to a district where they didn't think much or wish for much, but possessed great riches. I feasted with eyes that had become fond and strange upon the home things which were my own." Campbell's account of this period of his life goes on to dwell on the stone-building tradition of the area, a material he had not been able to use freely in the suburbs of German cities where he had worked until then. He was, however, aware of the limitations of working in these conditions, writing: "The photographs of my Cotswold work don't represent my thoughts and intentions but they represent all they can in the circumstances; an effort to use the old craftsman traditions that can still be found, and to learn from them for the future. Soon these traditions will not be here. Even now they are not quite real, and an architect must have a strong sense of reality."

Responding to this awareness, Campbell left Gloucestershire in 1923 and set up a London office of Falconer, Baker & Campbell at 27 Soho Square. He presumably hoped to attract the same kind of jobs he had enjoyed ten years earlier in

Germany. At the same time, the dating of his work from publications implies that he continued to be involved in the Cotswold work of the firm.

He tried to launch out with regional broadcasting buildings for the BBC which were cancelled at short notice when Campbell's patron within the organisation left suddenly. These surely show Campbell's concern for the timeless in the interesting context of modern technology. The interiors of Broadcasting House were designed in 1932 by a younger generation of architects including another "graduate" of Waring & Gillow, Serge Chermayeff, mostly in the Modern style.

Alterations and additions, garden design, Great Rissington Manor, Gloucestershire c.1925-26
The Manor House is typical of many Cotswold houses which have been progressively enlarged with a stylistic consistency which makes their history hard to unravel. At the core is a 17th century house to which at least one substantial addition seems to have been made before Campbell became involved. The client was Major W. P. Marling.

The available drawings do not completely explain the extent of Campbell's involvement. The forecourt and gates form part of his scheme, but probably not much of the exterior architecture seen on approach. Campbell planned to build a Great Hall to make a third side to the forecourt and link a pre-existing fragment of building to the main house. Although the designs were published this was not carried out. Internally there is much fine linenfold panelling in oak with very crisp carving and a built-in dresser in the dining room which relates to Campbell's pre-war German work.

The terraced garden looks down toward the River Windrush and Campbell's layout, including a pergola and gazebo, is his best piece of garden architecture in England, recalling some of the features of his German houses. The garden design is architectural, with a rectangular plan supported by retaining walls, marked to the south by a pergola supported on circular pillars of rough stone masonry, terminated by a decorative niche at one end and by a thatched gazebo at the other. This

Overleaf and above: Great Rissington Manor, gazebo, pergola and interior

is simple in form, rising at the corner of the raised terrace with its stone base modified into a circular cill, on which rises a timber window-stage in the form of a rotated square, capped by a conical thatched roof. The interior is fitted with bench seats. Across the terraced lawn, a small garden with a sunken pool is marked by the building up of a corner pier in the stone wall into a dovecot, a piece of miniature architecture in which the thin arrises of Cotswold stone slates are shown off. As a simple piece of abstract three-dimensional design it is particularly satisfying.

The pergola, which a later owner partly took down to prevent it from blocking light from the house, would have abutted the proposed Great Hall and perhaps have formed part of a promenade from an alternative entrance. A further link between house and garden is provided in the Garden Room with a fine trussed roof and stairway. An abstract two-tier circular fountain originally stood on a circular paved area adjoining this.

Rudolf Pfister wrote in *Baukunst* in 1928: "For someone who does not respond to the stone dove-cot or to the beautifully thatched little summer-house at Great Rissington manor, every word written here is wasted. But even such a person will find it difficult to ignore the simple technical perfection or to resist the immense appeal of dry stone walls as pergola columns or stone tiled roofs. ... Anyone who, when confronted by such charming gardens and terraces, asks whether or not they are "modern" is thinking like a boring schoolmaster and certainly not an artist!"

Picket House, Avening, Gloucestershire, c.1925
A relatively small house of thin coursed rubble with a thatched roof, big chimney stack and thatched loggia overlooking a garden pool. Re-roofed in tile after a fire and altered in other respects.

The Bear Inn Hotel, Rodborough Common, Stroud c.1925
A pre-existing small inn was enlarged on two sides, creating large-scale new accommodation suitable for the age of motor tourism. Campbell's design manages to let the two gables of the original building speak as part of an ascending scale to the four-storey bedroom wing which rises, castle-like, from the steeply falling land to the rear. This mass of building is actually an L - shape on plan, contributing one of five separate elements which make up a carefully-segregated set of buildings within the whole. These buildings, public house, tea room, restaurant, owner's appartments and kitchens, all have access through the irregularly-shaped courtyard, with its low-soffitted entrance disguised as an arch and covered way linking the separate parts.

PROPOSED MASONIC HALL : STROUD.
HALF INCH DETAIL OF FRONT ELEVATION :8

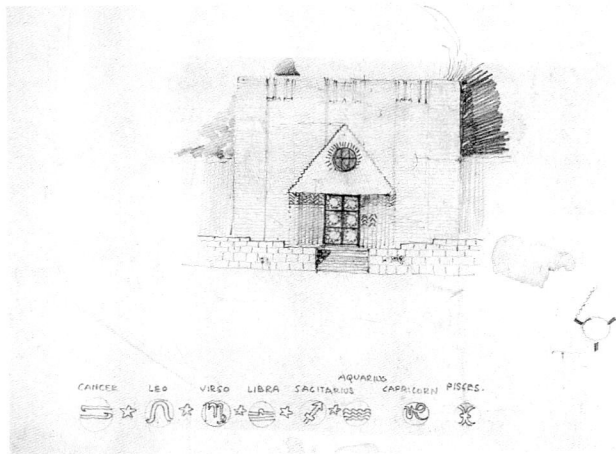

CANCER   LEO   VIRGO   LIBRA   SAGITARIUS   CAPRICORN   PISCES.

AQUARIUS

Project for Masonic Hall, Stroud, c.1924
This is one of Campbell's most striking designs and was no doubt considered too radical for its place and purpose. It is exceptionally public in its symbolic representation. The architectural forms of the elevation are reduced to elemental forms of square, triangle and circle to create architecture which is abstract rather than modern. While the simplicity may suggest aspects of the architecture of W. R. Lethaby, Campbell's design reflects the more austere aesthetics of the 1920s and the only comparable design of the time is Lloyd's Bank, Teddington by A. Randall Wells, 1927, who worked with Lethaby. England in the 1920s was not prepared for architecture of this power.

The inflection of pier and recessed bay in the windowless brick wall is expressed by different forms of indentation, with a frieze containing the signs of the zodiac with stars to space them out. Two preliminary sketches and a photograph of a finished elevation are the only records of the project. The latter is rendered in Campbell's typical "sinful" black pencil.

A Reinforced Concrete Church
Campbell built an elaborate model of this scheme, probably without any specific site in mind. It represents his attempt to re-enter the architectural mainstream, at a time when concrete was much under discussion as a building material. The triple nave recalls German hall churches while the web-like transverse arches resemble the aisles of St Jean de Montmartre by Anatole de Baudot, 1894–1904. The comparison most naturally drawn is with the churches of Auguste Perret, Notre Dame de

Raincy and St. Denis. Like these, Campbell uses the framing strength of concrete to have almost continuous glazed walls but the internal space is made more mysterious with the network of overhead arches, the two lines of columns and the transverse screens of columns and arches which show that even at his most modern, Campbell was concerned with the expressive qualities of space, specially in relation to a sacred building.

Maggs Bookshop interiors, 34-35 Conduit Street, London W1

This interior conversion in a simple Arts and Crafts style was supposed to suggest, by subtle prompts rather than overt stylistic reference, the historical period of the rare books kept in different parts of the shop, which were displayed with their fore-edges showing. The design of interiors and furnishings with bare surfaces is similar to the Minimalism of the 1990s.

The entire building was destroyed in the war.

ARLY IN THE YEAR 1929 Campbell returned to Berlin, tempted by offers of work from old friends and disillusioned with the lack of prospects in London. It was a time of economic prosperity in Germany, and Campbell could not know how soon this was to change in the wake of the 1929 Wall Street Crash. The article in the Munich-based *Baukunst* in June 1928 by the editor Rudolf Pfister must have been an added incentive, and Pfister called on him to provide a corrective of "unchanging truthfulness" to the rapidly changing fashions of Modernism.

If the dating of the Heinrich Mendelsohn house in Kladow to 1925-27, as recorded in the Historic Buildings Inventory for Berlin, is correct, then he must have renewed his contacts while still in London. For this project a number of drawings survive, although none correspond exactly with the house as built. Other surviving drawings from this period include several projects for the Golf Club house at Nedlitz, but the German magazines, so profuse in their coverage of Campbell's pre-war work, do not seem to have illustrated any projects from this later period.

Ein Golfhaus, Nedlitz, Saxony

The list of works is therefore dependent on the unpublished biography. This includes the completion of two projects left incomplete on the death of Campbell's old assistant, Eduard Pfeiffer, his house for the goldsmith Emil Lettre and Bussehaus. Pfeiffer's former assistant, Karl Hirschbold, joined Campbell during this period.

The project that one most wishes to see illustrated is the shop for Emil Lettre in Unter den Linden, in which this demanding patron pushed Campbell not into Modernism, but into a more austere and simplified style. It was destroyed in the war, as, apparently, were the best photographs of it. Campbell's biographer writes, "Design after design for the new front and interior of the shop was altered, re-considered and rejected. ... A small window was specified opposite the street door,

House for H. Mendelsohn.

through which the workmen could be seen at their benches; and it was necessary to protect it with bars. Campbell made "at least thirty drawings, each plainer than the last. In the end it was a single iron rod, most perfectly placed and proportioned, which spanned the opening from top to bottom."

An unnamed critic thought that it held "the absolute clue of architecture, based on and constructed by methods which were traditional but which represented a logical development through the complete fusion of our European culture with that of the East." By 1929 Modern Architecture was well-developed in Germany, although the magazines record buildings by pre-1914 architects which differ only by the refinement of detail and the use of veneered surfaces from their pre-war designs. Another critic wrote that Lettré's shop "caught the old and the new and mated them".

In hardly more than a year, Campbell had re-established himself in Berlin. He married for the second time in 1930; his wife, Frances Dagley, was the sister-in-law of Campbell's Ruhleben companion and London assistant, the Hon. Mark Kearley, second son of Lord Devonport. Frances was a furniture designer who ran her own workshop in Harrow.

The honeymoon gave Campbell the excuse for more extensive travels, to Paris, Barcelona, and an unspoilt Majorca. During the following year they also travelled to Arosa, Switzerland where Campbell made fine interiors for the Waldsanatorium, resembling contemporary work by Campbell's German contemporaries like Bruno Paul. The other project recorded in

photographs is the house for Baronness Rothschild on the Wannsee, near Berlin, a romantic, castle structure with a tower, an exercise in compositional massing recalling some of the hill towns and castles seen by Campbell in his travels in Germany and recorded in photographs and postcards. This house was taken up to a single storey height but abandoned late in 1931 when the rise of Nazism was becoming apparent.

Following the Wall Street Crash in October 1929, the financial situation in Germany deteriorated, leading to political disorder. The Campbells' flat in Victoriastrasse in the Embassy Quarter was subject to an 8p.m. curfew and every street entrance was guarded by lorries of police with searchlights and machine-guns. The Campbell's son, Colin, their only child, was born in July 1931. In October Frances and Colin left, followed by Campbell, who was unable to settle outstanding tax debts and left hurriedly by car, crossing a lonely frontier at night.

Waldsanatorium, Arosa, Graubunden, Switzerland

Chapel Point House, photo by John Campbell

THE FINAL PERIOD of Campbell's life as an architect took place in England and produced the buildings by which he is best known. It also led him to a more definite formulation of his architectural philosophy.

Campbell's first impulse was to find land on which to build a house for himself and his family, and he achieved this at Chapel Point between 1932 and 1935. This also became the first part of an experiment in small house design and construction by direct labour which drew together strands of his earlier experience to make what he considered a valid alternative to Modernism.

During this period of concentration on Chapel Point, Campbell designed and carried out one major building, the house Birchens Spring at Beaconsfield and one small house at Helston. Publication of the former in *Country Life* in 1938 brought Campbell back to public notice in England for the first time since the article in *Studio* in 1925, which in any case had been illustrated only by projects, not by actual buildings.

By this date, Christopher Hussey, the author of the article, was becoming disillusioned with much of the Modern architecture of England and found in Campbell a convincing alternative, someone re-opening pathways from thirty years earlier that had been prematurely closed by the strange movements of English taste.

He made designs for two speculative ventures with the developer H. Mendelsohn (no relation of the architect Eric Mendelsohn but probably the client of Campbell's Berlin house of the late 1920s). Although distinguished from the normal range of developer's architecture of the time, neither the scheme for flats at Chiswick Mall, nor the development of Marine Drive, Rottingdean, represent Campbell's best work. He also began designs for a cinema at Teignmouth. Campbell was working architecturally on his own during this period, although he shared the use of a London office. The narrative of Campbell's life in

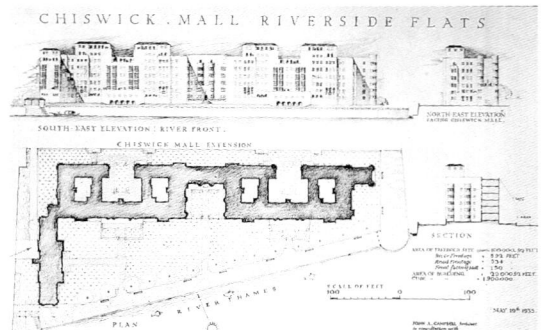

Project for flats, Chiswick Mall

these years is largely contained in the story of Chapel Point and need only be considered here in terms of the interval of the Second World War and architectural projects that followed it. During the war he worked briefly for the Ministry of Aircraft Production in London during 1940 before being invited to teach at Blundell's School, Tiverton. This remarkable episode is described in Ronald Leask's essay. A change of Headmaster caused him to leave in April 1944 and he then went to London to work for a church boys' club in Hoxton. There he viewed the prototype Portal House (a prefabricated steel house) on display at the Tate Gallery, causing him to compose a long letter to the *Builder* arguing in favour of perma-nent construction with traditional materials. Campbell spent the summer building The Ark at Chapel Point, in the company of his wife and son and then on his own.

In December 1944 Campbell established an office at 189 Brompton Road, over a dress shop run by his mother-in-law. After a period of inac-tivity, the publication of Chapel Point a few months after the end of war created a consider-able demand for houses from private clients. Many schemes were drawn up but it was almost impossible, in fact nearly illegal, to build anything. In this office he was assisted at times by his for-mer Blundell's pupil, Ronald Leask. Campbell designed another concrete church, for the rebuilding of All Saints, Chilvers Coton in the Diocese of Coventry, where Neville Gorton was Bishop. The project for building houses on the Island of Gigha as part of a scheme to re-establish a community under the new owner, Colonel Horlick was an attempt to construct a communi-ty with appropriate architecture.

All Saints, Chilvers Coton

The Chapel Point scheme was pursued with the elaborate model made for exhibition at the Royal Academy. This revived public interest in the proposal, although Campbell's plans for a fourth house, passed before the war and now intended as another house for his own family, were refused permission under the terms of the new Town and Country Planning Act. In late July and early August Campbell prepared an elab-orate appeal and completed and submitted it while on holiday at Chapel Point in his "Ark". It was later described by a Government official as "the most beautifully presented and the most painstakingly put together of any that I have seen". The appeal was successful but the house was never built, as it was on his return from post-ing this appeal document that Campbell fell from the cliff at night and was killed.

Model of Birchens Spring

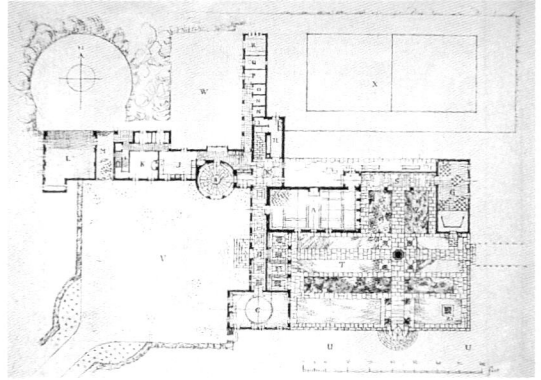

Birchens Spring Plan

Birchens Spring

The client of this country house was C. Rissik, a diamond merchant. The commission may have come through Frances Campbell's mother who lived near Gerrards Cross at Hawkswood, a house designed by Mark Kearley with a cardroom by Campbell. Rissik seems to have given a reasonably free rein to his architect and must have encouraged some of the elements of fantasy in the room shapes and plan-form. The house was bought by Dirk Bogarde after the war and renamed "Drummer's Yard" after a figure of a drummer-boy placed in the front courtyard. The name has been retained by subsequent owners, but the original name is used here.

Photographs of the model for the house show several variations to what was built, chiefly the orientation of the forecourt and wings and the inclusion of a circular space in the centre of the covered walk between the main house and the "playhouse". The latter feature is included in the contract drawings and must have been a late omission on grounds of cost.

The house stands on a new site, visible from the Beaconsfield-Amersham road, where the land slopes away to the east. The plan is spread out and creates the impression of an even larger house. The dominant impressions of the exterior are of the uniformity of white walls and slate roofs, not local materials. There are hardly any exterior architectural "features" and in this the house returns to the examples of Baillie Scott, with its round tower harking back to Scott's House for an Art Lover.

In terms of planning, Campbell's extended footprint, the consequence of following his mediaeval principle of "to every room a roof", enables the service court to be kept well away from the body of the house and made into an attractive feature in its own right. In contrast, therefore, to a conventional house with two main fronts, Birchens Spring offers a variety of aspects

on four sides and makes a series of semi-enclosed spaces around it, including the entrance court, the service court, the terraced garden by the house and the space to the rear where the rectangular "tower" appears at its strongest. A diagonal emphasis is introduced by the corner balcony on the tower, overlooking the raised garden terrace, which is partially enclosed by the "playhouse", a children's theatre reached by a covered way. The plan is therefore a linked series of pavilions, resulting in a generous proportion of circulation space, put to good use in creating an effect of individual character and privacy in the rooms. As Christopher Hussey pointed out in *Country Life* in

1938, Birchens Spring found a different architectural language for the modernist programme of out-door living, fresh air and sunlight, with the garden terrace envisaged as "a big summer-time extension of the house."

The openings in the white-painted brick (now covered with render) are varied in size, shape, depth of reveal and glazing patterns and materials. Round-headed openings and round blind tympani are mixed with square, and similar windows are subtly grouped.

The quality of internal light and the framing of external views are equally considered.

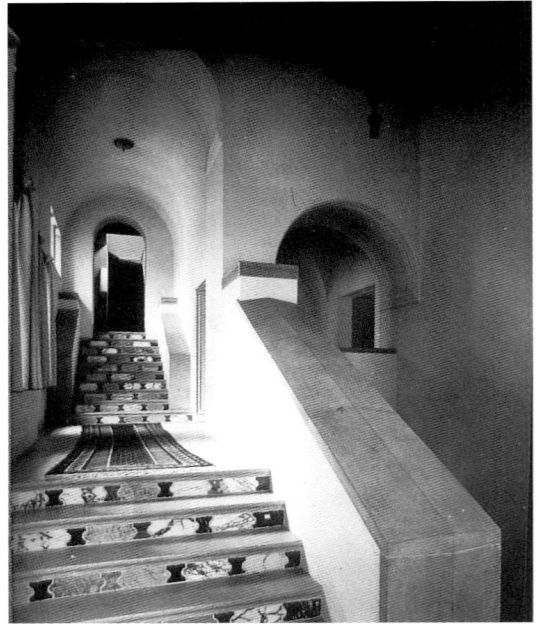

The two-storey entrance range belies its thinness on plan, for the front door leads into a corridor and directly out by a glazed door to the garden. The hallway is down the brick and stone barrell-vaulted passageway to the left, where the first flight of stairs disappears mysteriously into space with its richly coloured marble risers. The stair, with a solid balustrade capped by heavy coping stones, turns at a half landing and then offers a splendid perspective of views along corridors at two levels and up a further flight up to the second floor. Campbell's biographer comments, "when one stands at the foot of the staircase and looks upwards, an added meaning has been given to the word Space."

The hallway below gives access to the circular dining room in the tower facing the entrance and to the main living room, a higher space than the other rooms, with simple plaster mouldings, tall windows on the long side facing the garden and low windows with deep, plaster-moulded reveals on the short side. The fireplace has simple mouldings, showing off the tooling of the granite base and deep sandstone lintel. The doors of the ground floor rooms were made in walnut by the famous Cotswold cabinet-maker, Peter Waals (1870-1937).

Dirk Bogarde made internal alterations, as did his successor. The incised stone panel by John Farleigh over the fireplace of the drawing room, which is reached by turning right on entering the house, and the dining room murals by the client's brother, A. M. Rissik disappeared during this period. During recent extensive refurbishment work by the present owner many features have been restored using old photographs and surviving work as evidence, including plaster cornices, chimneypieces and new doors to replace missing original ones.

Chapel Point development, model, 1947. The three executed houses are in the foreground.

Chapel Point

Campbell wrote, "I believe that I can take the poor man's home and make it what it should be: honest and true and worthy of a man to live in it. I intend to try and break through the monstrous convention that 'architecture' is for the rich and jerry-building is for the rest. For if architecture is not for all, it is for none."

The initial intention was to build a single house for himself but owing to economic pressures, he built two more in the 1930s and planned a settlement in harmony with the natural beauty of the site.

Campbell initially built a temporary wooden hut which he occupied with his wife and child while building work began with direct labour. The education of the labourers was part of the wider mission of the project, and among other things Campbell taught the mason Arthur Ball to construct swept valleys in slate by direct demonstration. Stone was blasted on site and the house, Chapel Point House, gradually brought to habitable condition during 1935. Concrete blocks were made on site for the inner walls and Campbell also made cob for garden walls. The roofs are of grey-green Delabole slate with large slates at the eaves. Floors are also of riven slate, treated with linseed oil.

Chapel Point: Gatehouse and roofs of adjacent houses

Chapel Point House

The design of Campbell's own house evolved during the building process, becoming larger in the process, but it remained very simple and direct, based on a 10ft module on plan, the rooms fitting together logically but with elements of surprise in level and sequence of shape. Kitchen and study are both 10ft square. Only the cross-wing of the house is two-storey, containing a complete master-bedroom suite. The west-facing blank wall of the upper storey (blocking the prevailing wind) adds grandeur to the composition and sets off the low workshop wing, of lighter construction. The angle between these creates an entrance court, while the main rooms give onto a sheltered walled-garden.

Internally, Chapel Point House demonstrates Campbell's desire to use the roof space for the benefit of the room, with a boarded barrel-vault in the living room and the bedroom roof exposed up to the rafters. The internal openings are arched, creating attractive sequences of vistas. There is very little ornamental work and it is of the simplest kind, like the brick lattice pattern of the whitewashed study chimneypiece. In the living room, small bricks are exposed in the coving over

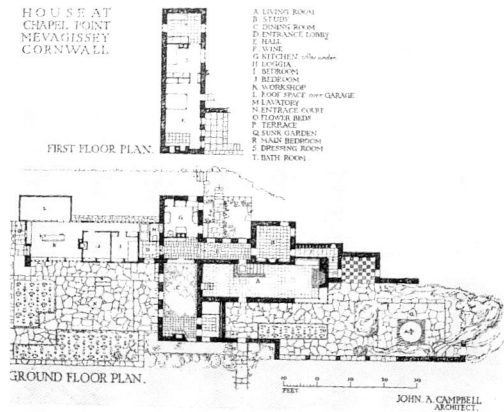

the settle recess. There is a play of levels, with the living room reached up a flight of six steps inside the space of the room, and the bedrooms up a half level again. At the entrance to the living room, a dramatic *coup d'oeuil* is given by the alignment of three arched openings looking out to sea. Campbell was obliged to sell his house during the war, but it deserves to stand in a sequence of twentieth-century architects' own programmatic and visionary houses.

Point Head Cottage

The smallest of the three Chapel Point houses, Point Head is on falling ground near the eastern tip of Chapel Point. The upper storey includes the living room, with kitchen-dining below, reached by a cross-passage hallway in mediaeval plan form. The large chimneystack rises on the long side of these rooms, with a coke store and boiler built around its base and adding solidity to the composition.

As at Chapel Point House, there is a substantial workshop attached to the house and overlooking the garden, which has a circular wall enclosing a singe large flower bed.

Christopher Hussey wrote, "The experiment in this case is in the combination of materials: the chimney, plinth and outbuildings are of rubble, but the main walls of concrete blocks ... As if to anchor the building to the rock-face, a massive chimney pins down the outer end of the house."

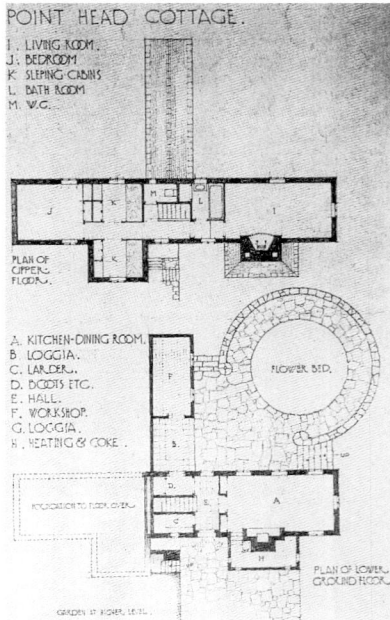

POINT HEAD COTTAGE.

I . LIVING ROOM.
J . BEDROOM
K . SLEEPING CABINS
L . BATH ROOM
M . W.C.

PLAN OF UPPER FLOOR.

A . KITCHEN-DINING ROOM.
B . LOGGIA.
C . LARDER.
D . BOOTS ETC.
E . HALL.
F . WORKSHOP.
G . LOGGIA.
H . HEATING & COKE .

FLOWER BED.

FOUNDATION TO FLOOR OVER.

PLAN OF LOWER GROUND FLOOR.

GARDEN AT HIGHER LEVEL.

three low windows of the living room to the single arch-headed window of the principal bedroom above. The peak of the gable is emphasised by thin projecting masonry courses and a narrow slit window to the attic. On the face of the wall triangular corbel stones encourage the tracing of imagined diagonal lines to establish proportional relationships.

The house does form a gateway to the other houses, overlooking the approach road which passes between curved stone walls While a grand entrance is provided, it is clear from the plan-form and orientation that the natural entrance is by the kitchen, reached through a courtyard whose corners are emphasised by turreted piers. This contained lean-to buildings on two sides with the kitchen filling most of the third side. The width of plan at ground level is reduced above, so that each roof spans only 15 ft, with an internal room width of 10ft, a comfortable width for conversation in the tall living room with its painted ceiling, originally executed by Campbell himself.

Gate House

The most elaborate architectural design of the three, the Gate House stands up highest on the point, its compactness of plan generating an upward movement. The tower-house form and balconies are closer in style to Birchens Spring than the other Cornish houses. On the entrance side the staircase is expressed by a semi-circular tower, into which a diagonal oriel is butted, a request of the client which Campbell regretted. The end elevation rises from a four-arched loggia, separating laterally into two compositions within one wall-plane, the main one reaching up past the

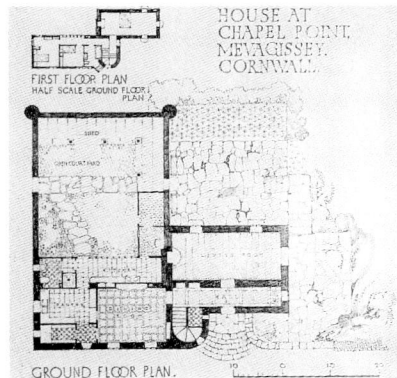

HOUSE AT
CHAPEL POINT,
MEVAGISSEY,
CORNWALL

FIRST FLOOR PLAN
HALF SCALE GROUND FLOOR
PLAN 2

GROUND FLOOR PLAN.

Pentyr, Helford

Built by Campbell in 1938 on the same principles as the Chapel Point houses and with the same craftsmen. The site is further west in Cornwall on an equally beautiful site on the south bank of the Helford River, a broad estuary with gently sloping tree covered banks. Pentyr is simple and unpretentious, but finely composed in mass and scale with a single long roof ridge and projecting wings. On the east side, a pair of dormers grouped with a solid chimney stack give just the sort of compositional pleasure that Philip Webb was able to achieve with simple elements.

The Ark

In 1944 Campbell bought a single-boarded chicken-hut from Tiverton which he had transported to Mevagissey. Two extra rooms were added to make a holiday home, with kitchen, living room and workshop. The construction work was undertaken almost entirely by Campbell himself, then aged sixty seven. His biographer wrote:

"The Ark was finished. It lay compactly on the ground, it was altogether clothed in bark, a true log cabin, and its windows were polished. I entered. ...There was nobody in it but in the fireplace a wood fire burned brightly and a kettle was singing on the hob. In front of the hearth Campbell's Windsor chair was drawn up, with a book lying face downwards on the seat. ... The whole arrangement was orderly, colourful, fresh, cheerful, welcoming and homely. ... it was not the appearance of the room that really arrested me, it was the sense of presence. The builder had become incorporated in his work. The room was at peace. It was in a state of wholeness. Here in the warm contained air was no before and no after, no question and no answer: a perfect fullness of life and present sufficiency. I went outside again and with the utmost concentration observed the three houses in the background, comparing their great white mass with the small black hut before me. It seemed to me that the houses pointed the way to the hut."